FAREWELL
TO NINIAN PARK

Dennis Morgan

To Les

Best wishes

Dennis Morgan

2008

Published by
DENNIS MORGAN
139 Carisbrooke Way,
Cyncoed,
CARDIFF
CF23 9HU
Telephone: (029) 2048 4034

Published by
DENNIS MORGAN
139 Carisbrooke Way,
Cyncoed,
CARDIFF
CF23 9HU

ISBN: 978-0-9534455-1-6

Printed by HSW Print, Tonypandy, Rhondda, CF40 2XX (01443) 441100

CONTENTS

FOREWORD BY
RICHARD SHEPHERD

Ninian Park Memories

Richard Shepherd is a former BBC Radio Wales and Independent Radio football commentator and is now Cardiff City's internet match commentator. He is also the club's historian and a member of the match magazine editorial team. He has been watching Cardiff City for over 50 years.

The end of Ninian Park – a sad and perhaps emotional time for anyone who has long memories of this old place. We all have recollections of players and games that stand out for us. I can still recall the first match I saw at this ground, a 3-2 home defeat by Portsmouth in Division I on 2 April 1956 in which players such as Trevor Ford, Gerry Hitchens and Ron Stitfall, all sadly no longer with us, took part.

That particular game doesn't form part of Dennis Morgan's excellent compilation and why should it? He has his own memories of matches that stand out for him, as well as relating tales from games long before World War II, matches that are an important part of City's history.

Promotions are always a highlight in one's memories of a club. I particularly recall the last time City gained promotion to Division I. It was Easter Saturday 1960 when Cardiff beat already promoted Aston Villa 1-0 to win promotion back to the top tier of the Football League. I can still visualise Graham Moore's goal at the Grange end in front of a crowd of 55,000, the biggest attendance in the country that day.

What pleases me about this book is that Dennis has paid due regard to the opposing teams and their personalities. He is a long-time Cardiff City supporter who wants his team to be successful but he also appreciates the talent and ability of the opposition – an appreciation that is perhaps sadly lacking among the current generation of football fans.

All of the games Dennis has recalled are well known to me in the course of my research. One particular game, where I was present, stands out. It was the "Greg Farrell" match against Middlesbrough in 1966. Winger Greg Farrell gave the performance of his life as City won 5-3 to ensure Second Division safety at the expense of their opponents. That display for me was the greatest individual performance I have ever seen from a Cardiff City player in over half a century of watching the club.

A new stadium lies ahead and the old place will be a fond memory for all of us. This excellent work by Dennis Morgan, a respected author on the City of Cardiff and its history, will be a tangible reminder of great games and memories connected with Ninian Park.

Richard Shepherd
July 2008

INTRODUCTION AND ACKNOWLEDGEMENTS

I was eight years old when I first saw Cardiff City play a wartime match against Bath City. A 5-2 defeat should have warned me what I was letting myself in for, but in1946 I became a regular supporter. For more than 60 years I have watched the City going through its ups and downs and I was present for virtually every game I have written about since 1945.

The book is about the history of this famous ground, now nearing the end of its days and some of the significant matches played there through the years. Others may disagree with my choice but, while the games I have chosen are not necessarily the greatest matches seen at Ninian Park, they were all significant in the fortunes of Cardiff City and Wales. I have written from a fan's viewpoint and my research is largely based on my personal memories and diaries, as well as the programmes and newspapers I have been collecting since I was 11 years old.

At the same time I am indebted to other people for helping me in my work. I would like to offer my appreciation to the staff in the Local Studies Department of the Central Library for their very courteous and helpful attitude when I have carried out my research. In seeking background information I found Grahame Lloyd's book, *C'mon City* and John Crooks's *Official History of Cardiff City* valuable aids

Many individuals have contributed to my selection of photographs, including those chosen from Stewart Williams' *Cardiff Yesterday* series. In particular, Cardiff City AFC and the *Western Mail and Echo* have been most generous in allowing me access to their superb collection.

I must pay a special tribute to Richard Shepherd who has been kind enough to read the proofs prior to publication and to write the foreword for me. As the archivist and historian of Cardiff City, he has written several books about the club. Many of my illustrations, especially the older programmes, come from his extensive collection of archive material about the Bluebirds. He has offered suggestions, answered my queries, and allowed me to draw on his considerable knowledge for assistance and advice.

I am grateful to HSW Print for their help in producing this book. Wayne Biddle has given me sound advice, not for the first time, in overcoming the practical problems of self-publishing. My family has always been a great help to me in the writing of my books. Six members of us, drawn from three generations, are now Cardiff City season ticket holders and they know this particular work was a labour of love. Whenever I have needed it they have given me encouragement and help. I apologise if I have inadvertently overlooked the contribution anyone else has made to my work and hasten to add that any errors remaining in the text are entirely mine. Finally, I hope that these pages will bring back some nostalgic memories for those reading them.

THE EARLY YEARS AT NINIAN PARK

From Riverside to Cardiff City

The Riverside Football Club was inspired by Bartley Wilson who, despite being crippled with a club foot, was a keen sportsman. In 1899, as secretary of the Riverside Cricket Club, he proposed, as a means of keeping players together in the winter, the formation of a football team. Its first match against Barry West End ended in a 9-1 defeat but, undaunted, in the following year Riverside entered the Cardiff and District League. The team played its matches at Sophia Gardens or the Harlequins' ground in Roath.

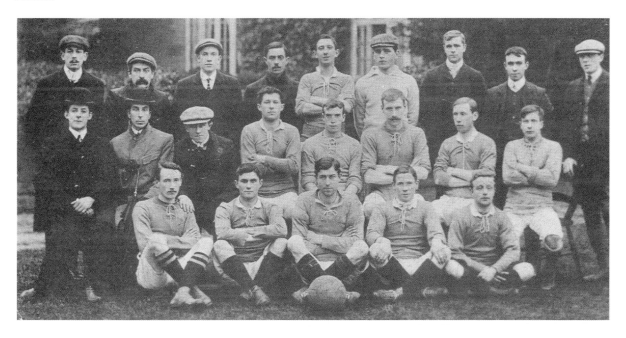

Bartley was certain there was scope in Cardiff for a football team capable of playing at a far higher level than the local league. His determination to achieve this goal led to a lifelong association with the club he had founded which continued until his death in 1954. A week after Cardiff was designated a city in October 1905, Bartley applied to the South Wales and Monmouthshire FA for permission to change Riverside's title to "Cardiff City". The request proved to be premature. First it was necessary for the club to play in a higher grade of football so Riverside entered the South Wales League in 1906. Playing against teams such as Newport, Aberdare and Ton Pentre, the team lost far more matches than it won, one game against Ton Pentre ending in an 8-2 thrashing.

An early photograph of Riverside Football Club, taken at Sophia Gardens. Bartley Wilson is in the back row, second from the left.

The club's colours were originally chocolate and amber quarters but in 1908 it changed its strip to the familiar blue. In November 1911 a play entitled *The Blue Bird* was performed at the New Theatre and, following publicity in the local press, supporters began to cry at Ninian Park, "Come on, you blue birds". The nickname "Bluebirds" has remained ever since

However, on 5 September 1908 at the Alexandra Hotel in Queen Street, permission was finally given for Bartley's team to be renamed "Cardiff City". The club was warned that, "if a professional team should be started in Cardiff in the near future, they would relinquish the name".

Bartley Wilson in his eighties, sorting international tickets with his son, Jim (centre), and club secretary, Trevor Morris.

Wilson had no intention of allowing anyone else to thwart the ambition he now envisaged for Cardiff City. Aberdare, Merthyr and Treharris were already playing in the Southern League with gates often above 10,000. He had no doubt that there was similar enthusiasm in Cardiff but, in order to progress, the club needed its own enclosed stadium. Early in 1910 the search began for a suitable ground.

Bartley approached the Bute Estate to see if land was available on Leckwith Common, now about to become the site of Cardiff City's new stadium. While these discussions were proceeding, John Mander, a leading councillor, suggested that a former allotments site and rubbish tip on Sloper Road might be an alternative. He also promised that the Council would give as much support as it could. Bartley wrote a number of letters to the Parks Department, requesting that five acres of this rough land should be converted into an enclosed stadium. He suggested a 14 year lease and an initial ground rent of £60 a year, eventually rising to a maximum of £100.

The club's offer was accepted but there was a condition. Cardiff City had to provide guarantors for the ground rent. At first this was not easy but five were eventually found. The most prominent of these was Lord Ninian Crichton Stuart, the second son of the Marquis of Bute. In his honour the club decided to name the new ground "Ninian Park".

A limited company was formed on 21 April 1910 with seven directors and Bart Wilson as secretary. Soon afterwards the club was admitted to the Second Division of the Southern League for the 1910-11 season which left only three months to form a team and prepare the ground for its first game. The Board of Directors was given greater credibility in June when the original seven resigned and among their replacements were Sid Nicholls, the Cardiff rugby forward who became chairman, and Joseph Brain, an ex-Glamorgan cricket captain.

Preparing the ground for its first match was a huge task. A member of the former Riverside team, Jack Finn, acted as groundsman. With the aid of numerous volunteers, the pitch was levelled and the surplus soil was heaped around it. The Council's Refuse Department, the gasworks on Penarth Road and local factories all provided ashes, clinker and other material to build up raised banks on the sides of the ground. When a stiff breeze was blowing, spectators in those early days often returned home covered in dust. If it was wet they could be ankle deep in slurry. The teams shared a dressing room at the Canton end of the ground and, as there was no running water, bowls of water were heated on a coal-fired stove. The office was also situated in this area and, along the Sloper Road side of the stadium, a small wooden grandstand with a canvas roof provided seating for 200 spectators. Before the end of August 1910 the ground was enclosed and ready for its first game.

Lord Ninian Crichton Stuart, MP for Cardiff, war hero and guarantor of Cardiff City's ground rent. He was known as, "a downright good sport, as happy among working men as he was in a duchess's drawing room".

Training at Ninian Park before the 1910-11 season. A great deal of work remained to be done before its official opening. Notice the railway signal box, the ash covered banks and the primitive fencing.

The pitch was not only rough but remnants of glass and other dangerous objects from the former rubbish dump worked their way to the surface. On the morning of a match players were paid 6d an hour to remove this debris. Even so, there were casualties when players fell. Jack Evans was one victim when he fell on a piece of glass and his knee was scarred for life. The career of Peter McWilliam, the Scottish and Newcastle wing half, was ended in March 1911 when he suffered a similar fate. That game between Wales and Scotland was the first international match to be played at Ninian Park.

The ground still had a primitive appearance but its capacity had risen to 17,000. Facilities were improving as gas and a much needed water supply were connected to the manager's office and the dressing rooms. Alongside Sloper Road, players and supporters began work on a wooden grandstand, large enough to hold 2,000 spectators. In little more than a decade since he had formed the Riverside club, the drive and enthusiasm of Bartley Wilson was being fulfilled.

In December 1910 a 5,000 crowd watched this Welsh Cup-tie against Ton Pentre. By now the playing area was enclosed though spectators are standing inside the railings. The match ended in a 2-2 draw and City lost the replay 1-0.

The Inaugural Match: Thursday 1 September 1910

Cardiff City (0) 1 Aston Villa (2) 2

For the official opening of Ninian Park, Cardiff City arranged a friendly match with Aston Villa. They could scarcely have chosen more prestigious opponents as the Villa had won the FA Cup four times and were the current Football League Champions. The team selected to play Cardiff was a strong side though many of the players were reserves. George, a burly goalkeeper, Layton and Kearns had played regularly in Villa's successful side the previous season. The *Western Mail* observed that the "Villans" were capable of putting two teams in the field, either of which could compete in the First Division.

Jack Evans from Bala became Cardiff City's first professional player in June 1910. He believed his playing days were over when he damaged his shoulder while playing for Wrexham. He moved to South Wales to look for work and began playing football again for Cwmparc-and-Treorchy United before Bartley Wilson persuaded him to sign for Cardiff. He was only paid 35/- a week but the promise of a part-time job with the Imperial Printing Company was enough to tempt him. He was one of the best signings the club ever made. He was renowned for his powerful shooting and so successful was the resumption of his football career that he went on to win eight caps for Wales.

Jack Evans, the City's first professional player. He played for the club until 1926, sharing in the glory days of the 1920s.

After signing Jack Evans, Bartley Wilson's next move was to appoint Davy McDougall from Glasgow Rangers as player-manager. Before the start of the 1910-11 season McDougall had signed 14 professionals, a clear indication that the amateur days were over and Cardiff meant to be a force in the Southern League. Most of these newcomers came from Scotland or the North of England though the goalkeeper, Ted

Husbands, joined the club from Wrexham. The players had little time to prepare for the coming season. Only a couple of practice matches were possible against local amateur teams before the big game against Aston Villa.

The programme for the official opening match at Ninian Park shows Cardiff City's first professional squad and the team for the game with Aston Villa.

CARDIFF'S FIRST PROFESSIONAL SOCCER TEAM.
(READ LEFT TO RIGHT.)
R. PEAKE, J. MACKENZIE, E. HUSBANDS, J. EVANS, J. DUFFY, W. STEWART,
J. MACDONALD, R. LAWRIE, D. M'DOUGALL, J. L. RAMSEY, T. ABLEY,
W. WATTS, J. MALLOCH

Lord Ninian Stuart was the guest of honour for this opening match and also present were members of the City Council and prominent local businessmen. A crowd of more than 5,000 were in the ground when Lord Ninian made a short speech, wishing the club well. He then declared the ground open and made the ceremonial kick-off at 5 p.m.

A grainy but historic photograph, showing Lord Ninian Stuart kicking off against Aston Villa to officially open the ground.

It was not long before the Villa showed their class as they took the lead in the 8th minute. Eyre crossed the ball to **Whittaker** who beat Husbands with a low shot. Though George in the Villa goal was tested a couple of times, it was Cardiff's goalkeeper, Husbands, who kept the score down with several fine saves. Just before half-time he was left helpless as a wide open City defence allowed **Walker** to score a second goal.

Cardiff began the second half strongly and the Villa goalkeeper was kept busy. However, the save of the match came from Husbands, when Hunter unleashed a tremendous shot from 40 yards which the City goalkeeper kept out with a dive to his right. The Bluebirds never gave up and two minutes from time the honour of scoring their first goal at Ninian Park fell to **Jack Evans**, the only Welshman in the team. He broke down the left and, after outpacing Layton, he hammered the ball home from 15 yards.

The cover of the programme for the inaugural match. Who would have thought that, just over ten years later, the two sides would be meeting in a First division game?

So ended the first major event at Ninian Park. *Citizen*, writing in the *Western Mail*, gave the performance a mixed reception. There was honour in defeat and nothing to make "even the most timid believer in signs and portents downhearted". The crowd of 7,000 for this first game was encouraging but the performance against Aston Villa needed considerable improvement. The forwards lacked finishing power, while the blunder in defence which led to the second goal "was well nigh criminal". The Villa had been given a clear run on goal and Lawrie, the right half, "appeared to have gone on his holidays". He praised the goalkeeping of Ted Husbands who made many fine saves, while Jack Evans showed great promise.

Fred Stewart was the Bluebirds' first secretary-manager. His salary was £4 a week but he found enough time to carry on a successful corn and seed business.

A week later, the same writer was much more complimentary when the Bluebirds defeated Ton Pentre 3-2 in their opening match in the Southern League. He emphasised the difference between a friendly and a competitive match and, writing in a style typical of Edwardian Britain, was "convinced that Cardiff City can hold their own in that station of life which they are called upon to fulfil". This proved to be a more balanced view as the Bluebirds ended their first season in the Southern League in fourth place.

Southern League Division II: Saturday 2 September 1911

Cardiff City (3) 3 Kettering Town (0) 1

In May 1911 Cardiff appointed Fred Stewart as a full time secretary/manager. For 18 years he had been a part-time manager at Stockport County but he saw a greater potential at Cardiff, even though Stockport was a Football League club. Fred remained with the City for 22 years and became its most successful manager.

Billy Hardy never won the England cap most people felt he deserved but he had no regrets: "It was a small price to pay for being part of a very good Cardiff City side".

Before the commencement of the 1911-12 season, Stewart made several signings from Scotland and the North of England, thus indicating his knowledge of that area. He proved his ability for finding outstanding talent by signing Billy Hardy from Hearts. The fee was a mere £25 but, as the club's funds could not meet that figure, Fred paid it out of his own pocket and was reimbursed the following season. Billy was to play a major role in the Bluebirds' fortunes for the next 20 years. Playing at left half and only 5 feet 6 inches tall, he was a magnificent header of the ball. Hardy never played for England because the FA refused to consider capping a player from a Welsh club.

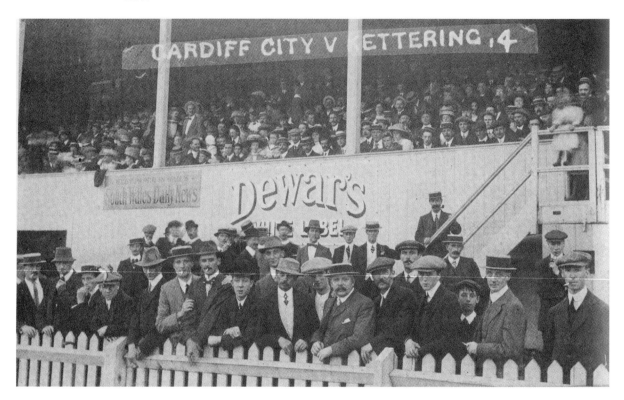

Well-dressed supporters are enjoying the game with Kettering in front of the new stand. In those days no-one had thought of the need for a ban on smoking.

The pitch had been remade, though a long drought gave it a parched appearance for the opening match against Kettering. The glorious summer weather was, according to one pundit, "more suitable for a channel cruise than a game of football". Nevertheless, in the first half the crowd of 6,000 had plenty to cheer about as the City outplayed their opponents with some excellent football. Kettering were rarely out of their own half and, after a number of near misses, Cardiff took the lead after 25 minutes through **Jack Burton** who was one of Stewart's summer signings. Another of his acquisitions, right winger Harry Tracey, forced a corner a few minutes later and, from the goalmouth scramble that followed, **Tom Abley** netted the second goal. Just before half-time **Tracey**, who had given the Kettering full back a torrid time, burst through the Kettering defence to score a third.

With the game virtually won, the pace slackened in the second half. City continued to be on top despite the heat and might have added further goals through Tracey and Jack Evans. Not until late in the game did Kettering produce their best spell of the afternoon and, in the dying minutes, **Parker** scored a consolation goal with a shot from close range which gave Husbands no chance.

In his comments, *Citizen* named Billy Hardy as the "star artiste", an accolade he would earn on many occasions in the future. Cardiff did not win promotion that season but managed a creditable third place. The team also wrote a new page in their brief history by defeating Pontypridd 3-0 in April 1912 to win the Welsh Cup for the first time. It was third time lucky the following year as Cardiff won promotion by finishing Second Division champions. The crowds at Ninian Park were becoming larger and to meet this demand the directors decided to extend the Grandstand along the entire length of the pitch.

The Bluebirds enjoyed two years in the First Division of the Southern League, finishing third in the 1914-15 season, before full time football gave way to the much more serious business of defeating the Kaiser. The only fatality of the war among the players was a reserve full back, Tom Witts, though sadly Lord Ninian Stuart, MP for Cardiff, who had done so much to help the club in 1910, lost his life to a sniper's bullet at the Battle of Loos.

Cardiff City team: Husbands; Waters, Leah; Lawrie, Thompson, Hardy; Tracey, Burton, Featherstone, Abley, Evans.

In this team photograph of 1914-15, the three players at the back were all victims of the Great War. Tom Witts (left) was killed in action and John Stephenson and Fred Keenor (right) were both wounded.

The cover of the programme for the Tottenham match. The artist's impression of the ground at that time shows the Grandstand and to its right the newly opened Canton Stand.

GREAT DAYS OF THE 1920S

When football returned to normality after the Great War, Cardiff City spent only one more year in the Southern League. Before the 1920-21 season the Football League was enlarged with a new Third Division. It was decided that Lincoln and Grimsby, the bottom clubs in Division II, should be relegated and Cardiff City and Leeds United were elected to take their place. The Bluebirds were fortunate in being allowed to start their Football League odyssey in the Second Division but immediately justified their election by winning promotion. The club then enjoyed the greatest period in its history, culminating in FA Cup glory at Wembley in 1927. The 1920s were also successful years for the national team.

Football League Division I: Saturday 27 August 1921

Cardiff City (0) 0 Tottenham Hotspur (0) 1

As Cardiff prepared for life among England's football elite, improvements were made to the stadium. The dressing rooms in the Grandstand were replaced and work on the new Canton Stand, with seating for 5,500 on its wooden benches, was completed in time for the new season.

The opening match was a very attractive fixture against the FA Cup holders, Tottenham Hotspur. The programme notes indicated the size of the challenge facing City by pointing out the depth of talent in the Spurs' team. Most of the City players chosen for this match had played for the club in the Southern League and the manner in which they adapted to a higher grade of football was a tribute to Fred Stewart's judgement. Yet Stewart was also aware of the need to strengthen the team and one of his shrewdest acquisitions was Jimmy Gill, signed from Sheffield Wednesday. During the previous season, he was the leading scorer in the Bluebirds' team that won promotion.

Fans had been eagerly anticipating the City's first match in Division I. By mid-day, when the turnstiles were opened, all roads leading to Ninian Park were packed with supporters who had travelled from all parts of South Wales. The gates were closed well before 3 o'clock with thousands of people still outside. A surge of spectators burst through the gates at the Canton end and forced many in the crowd to spill on to the pitch. The more venturesome occupied the girders of the Canton Stand while others climbed on to the roof of the Grandstand.

In the *Western Mail, Citizen* claimed there might have been as many as 60,000 present but astonishingly no-one was seriously hurt. It was a scene similar to that of the first Wembley Cup Final but, despite the horde of spectators surrounding the pitch only once, when Grimshaw took a corner, did the referee order them to retreat.

To quote that well worn cliché, the match itself was "a game of two halves". In the first 45 minutes the City defence, especially Keenor, Smith and Hardy, held the

OUR VISITORS.

This afternoon the Citizens embark upon their first season of 1st. Div. football confident in the knowledge that they have more than held their own with all of the premier division clubs with which they have come in contact and their victories over Sunderland and Chelsea last season, and Oldham the season before, together with the fact that many of the players have already figured prominently in English League games with other clubs, should materially assist in gaining for them as prominent a position in their present sphere as that gained in the old Southern League days.

A more difficult match with which to start the present campaign it would be hard to find, for the 'Spurs, in the opinion of many, last season proved themselves to be the finest team of the year, not even excluding the League Champions, Burnley, for whilst the latter towards the end of the season failed to show the form which marked their displays earlier on, the 'Spurs wound up in great style, carrying off the English Cup by defeating Wolverhampton Wanderers (the City's opponents in the semi-final) by 1-0 at Stamford Bridge, and finishing up in a prominent position in the League.

By a strange coincidence, the Citizens' last opponents last season were the Wolves, and their first opponents this season the 'Spurs, both last season's Cup Finalists, but whilst the Wolves were forced to acknowledge defeat in the Midlands by 3-1 it would be an extreme optimist who would expect the Citizens to register such an easy victory over the redoubtable 'Spurs.

The team to represent the Londoners is not expected to differ much, if at all, from the side which fielded regularly and proved so successful last season, and in this respect a big advantage is derived by the players knowing intimately each other's style of play.

In their first engagement the eleven is likely to consist of :—

HUNTER (goalkeeper)—The ex-Queen's Park (Glasgow) amateur, who by his brilliant displays eventually displaced Jacques, and won for himself an English Cup medal in his first season in English football.

CLAY (right back)—Reckoned to be one of the finest backs playing ; was capped for England against Wales in 1920.

MACDONALD (left back)—Since his inclusion with Clay has developed into a great player, the understanding between the pair being near perfect

SMITH (right half)—Secured by the Londoners from Huddersfield Has improved rapidly

since being with the 'Spurs, and last season was capped against Scotland

WALTERS (centre half)—Now occupies the position formerly occupied by Rance, who has departed to Derby County. Immediately "made good," and is now a regular member of the side.

GRIMSDELL (left half)—Needs no introduction, being a well-known figure in the realms of football Secured originally from Watford, and has developed until he is now considered to be one of the finest halves in the country Capped last season against Scotland and Ireland.

WALDEN (outside right)—A veritable box of tricks. First came into prominence with Northampton. Was absent from the side for a considerable period last season through injury, but is now fit and well, and expected to exhibit his old form at an early period

SEED (inside right)—An exceptionally clever forward whom the 'Spurs picked up whilst he was playing with Mid-Rhondda. His consistently good play soon won for him his place in the first team.

CANTRELL (centre forward)—Before appearing with the cup holders played with great success for Notts County. A clever leader, he has the happy knack of getting the best out of the men alongside him, beside being himself capable of frequently finding the net,

BLISS (inside left)—The marksman of the team. Last season scored on no fewer than 17 occasions. Has a tremendous shot with either foot. Selected, along with Dimmock, to play for England v Scotland last season, but failed to play up to club form.

DIMMOCK (outside left)—A splendid winger, was discovered locally, and quickly made a favourable impression in English League football. Is fast and tricky, besides being a dangerous shot. Will be remembered as having scored the all-important goal in last season's cup final, which secured for the Spurs' the coveted trophy.   LANCET.

GROUND IMPROVEMENTS

The ground has undergone considerable improvement during the close season. No doubt the most necessary has been the re-turfing of the playing pitch. This has been done with sea-washed turf by expert men, the pitch now being equal to the best in the country. An appeal is therefore made to all *not to run over the field after the match.*

Thousands of tons of ashes, etc., have been utilised to improve the banks, especially at the Grangetown end of the ground, whilst the new stand has been covered and many other improvements executed at a cost involving thousands of pounds.

The programme notes review Cardiff's opening match in the First Division. Few teams at that time were more welcome than the Cup holders, Tottenham Hotspur.

talented Tottenham forward line so well that Jack Kneeshaw was scarcely troubled. It was Hunter at the other end who was kept busy as he denied the City forwards what appeared to be certain goals at least three times. One save, a header from Fred Pagnam, was described by *Citizen* as "a super human effort". Yet half-time came with the scores still level.

In the second half the Bluebirds failed to reach the heights they had shown earlier. The Spurs' defence was much tighter and gradually it was their forwards who took command. The only goal of the game came from a clever inter-passing movement between Seed and **Banks** who was a late replacement for Walden on the right wing. His low shot gave Kneeshaw no chance and the appeals of City players for offside fell on deaf ears.

Despite their defeat Cardiff had played well enough to suggest they could make an impact in Division I. However, that appeared an unlikely scenario after the team lost its six opening matches. The recovery began on the last Saturday in September when the Bluebirds defeated the League leaders, Middlesbrough, 3-1. By the end of the season the team had risen to fourth place in the table, a very satisfactory beginning to their first season in the top flight.

Teams:
Cardiff City; Kneeshaw; Brittan, Page; Keenor, Smith, Hardy; Grimshaw, Gill, Pagnam, West, Evans.
Tottenham Hotspur: Hunter; Clay, Macdonald; Smith, Walters, Grimsdell; Banks, Seed, Cantrell, Bliss, Dimmock.

Some of the crowd who saw the match with Spurs. "Amazing scenes at Ninian Park" was how the Western Mail summed up the atmosphere at the game.

The Cardiff City team that played Spurs. Back row (left to right): Bert Smith, Billy Hardy, Jack Kneeshaw, George West, Jack Evans; Middle row: Billy Grimshaw, Jimmy Gill, Fred Pagnam, Charlie Brittan; Front row: Jack Page, Fred Keenor.

Home International Championship:
Saturday 16 February 1924

Wales (0) 2 Scotland (0) 0

Keenor (right) and Blair toss up before the game between Wales and Scotland. Notice that both players are wearing Cardiff City socks as their respective nations only provided shirts and shorts in those days.

It was claimed that attendances at international matches in South Wales often showed apathy among the local sporting public. Yet, for this 44th meeting between Wales and Scotland, a healthy crowd of about 30,000 were present. Cardiff City were enjoying a successful season and this may have attracted many to the game.

Unusually, the two captains, Fred Keenor and Jimmy Blair, both played for the City and there was a huge cheer as they tossed for ends. One of four Cardiff players on the field, Blair signed for the club in November 1920. The City had paid Sheffield Wednesday the considerable sum of £3,500 to obtain the 32 year old Scottish full back and for five years he and his fellow countryman, Jimmy Nelson, formed one of the best full-back partnerships in the Bluebirds' history.

It was 21 years since the Scots had won on Welsh soil but they dominated the early stages with accurate close passing. Had they scored at this point the result might have been different but their finishing did not match the approach work. The Welsh defence, especially Keenor and Billy Jennings, was superb and Albert Gray in the Welsh goal was rarely troubled. It was clear by half-time that the speedy Welsh forwards, especially Willie and Len Davies, were causing problems for the Scottish defenders and, of the two captains, Keenor was enjoying a happier afternoon than Blair.

The first half ended with honours even and, while Scotland again began strongly in the second half, it was **Willie Davies**, playing magnificently in his first international, who scored the opening goal for Wales. He received the ball just inside the Scottish half and outpaced Blair to beat Harper with a cross shot from just inside the penalty area. The Scots fought hard for an equaliser but it was Cardiff's **Len Davies** who put the result beyond doubt with a second goal after Harper failed to clear a cross from Richards. *Citizen*, writing in the *Western Mail*, said the game was, "a glorious exhibition of classical soccer" with never a dull moment.

Len Davies causes the Scottish defence an anxious moment as he heads towards goal in the international with Scotland.

It was the start of a great international campaign for Wales. A couple of weeks later, on a treacherous, half frozen pitch at Blackburn, Keenor was again in brilliant form as Wales defeated England 2-1. On 15 March, in a hard fought match at Belfast, Cardiff City's Tom Farquharson was in goal for Ireland but he failed to save a penalty. It was enough to give Wales a 1-0 victory and for the first time Wales had beaten all the home countries to win football's equivalent of the Triple Crown. Unfortunately, the Welsh success meant that Cardiff City had to play much weakened teams on two of these international occasions and dropped three valuable points in their chase for the First Division Championship.

Teams:

Wales: Gray (Oldham); Russell (Plymouth), Jenkins (Brighton); Herbie Evans (Cardiff), Keenor (Cardiff), Jennings (Bolton); Willie Davies (Swansea), Jones (West Bromwich Albion), Len Davies (Cardiff), Richards (West Ham), Vizard (Bolton).

Scotland: Harper (Hibernian); Marshall (Llanelly), Blair (Cardiff); Meiklejohn (Rangers), McBain (Everton), Muirhead (Rangers); Archibald (Rangers), Russell (Airdrieonians), Cassidy (Celtic), McKay (Blackburn), Morton (Rangers)

This was the Welsh team that played Scotland. Back row (left to right); Herbie Evans, Ivor Jones, Moses Russell, Bert Gray, Jack Jenkins, Bill Jennings; Front row: Billy Davies, Len Davies, Fred Keenor, Dick Richards, Teddy Vizard.

Football League Division I: Saturday 26 April 1924

Cardiff City (0) 2 Birmingham City (0) 0

The 1923-24 season saw the Bluebirds soar to heights they had never previously achieved even though the campaign had a disappointing finale. Before the last home game against Birmingham, Cardiff sat proudly on top of the First Division, level on points with Huddersfield Town but with a slightly better goal average. However, with a game in hand, Huddersfield still seemed favourites to take the title.

Rain was falling steadily when the game began but, considering the importance of the occasion, the crowd was a disappointing 18,000. The game was fairly even for 20 minutes and then Birmingham's fullback, Frank Womack, was taken off after an accidental clash of heads with Jimmy Gill. He played no further part in the game and the handicap of being a man short proved to be too much for Birmingham, though somehow the "gallant ten" held the Bluebirds at bay until half-time

Cardiff dominated the second half and within 10 minutes Gill cleverly held off two opponents before passing to Joe Clennell. He was able to find an unmarked **Jimmy Jones** who beat Dan Tremelling with a low shot. The City forwards now laid siege to

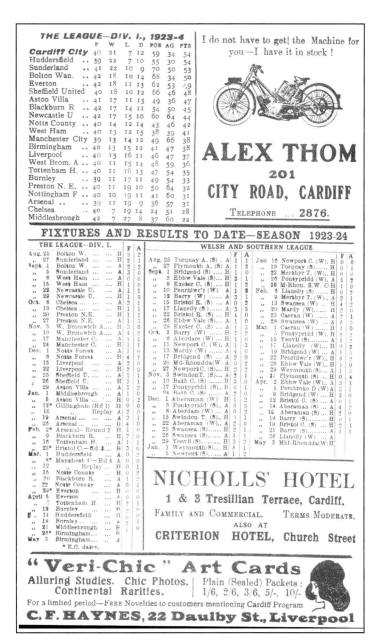

This page in the programme for the Birmingham match shows the Bluebirds' progress through the 1923-24 season. A miserable set of results in March was to cost them the First Division Championship.

the Birmingham goal and twice Gill was thwarted by brilliant saves from Tremelling. He was playing like a man inspired but should have been given no chance when Gill missed an open goal from close range.

The rain had now turned into a torrential downpour and players found it difficult to keep their feet on the greasy surface. With five minutes to go, Cardiff sealed their victory with a second goal. Jack Evans put across a perfect centre and **Clennell** fired a powerful shot past the gallant Tremelling.

Despite the appalling weather conditions, the game was described in the *Western Mail* as "one of the most interesting of the season". Cardiff should have won the match by a higher margin but Tremelling was in outstanding form. His heroics and the failure of the City forwards to make the most of their chances would come back to haunt them a week later.

A JOLLY GOOD ONE, TOO.

CARDIFF CITY CONJUROR: That, ladies and gentlemen, is the last rabbit I shall have the pleasure of producing from this hat this season.
On Saturday Cardiff City played their last home League match of the season.

J.C. Walker's optimistic cartoon after the City's victory against Birmingham but disappointment was to follow in the return match a week later.

Huddersfield had only managed to draw at Nottingham Forest and matters became even better for Cardiff a few days later when Huddersfield lost their match in hand 3-1 to Aston Villa. On the last day of the season the Bluebirds travelled to Birmingham for the return game with a one point advantage over Huddersfield. If they won they would be champions. Even a draw might be enough as Cardiff enjoyed a slightly superior goal average.

Len Davies who missed the vital penalty that would have brought the Championship to Wales. No-one else wanted to take it but the memory haunted Len for the rest of his days.

A crowd of nearly 50,000 watched this climax to the most exciting Championship race in League history. The City missed several chances to score but ten minutes from the end a header from Gill was goal bound when it was handled by full-back Barton. Jimmy Blair asked Len Davies to take the penalty as Jack Evans and Gill had recently missed from the spot. Len shot straight at Tremelling and the game ended in a 0-0 draw.

Soon the news arrived that Huddersfield had beaten Nottingham Forest 3-0. The teams were level on points with an identical goal difference. Huddersfield led Cardiff by 0.024 of a goal but it was enough to take the First

Division Championship to Yorkshire by the smallest margin in its history. Huddersfield Town were the outstanding team of the 1920s. Under their charismatic manager, Herbert Chapman, they won the First Division Championship in three successive years but Dame Fortune certainly smiled on them in 1924.

When the City players returned to Cardiff that evening, a crowd of several thousand welcomed them at the station. Len Davies probably never forgot that costly penalty miss but he and the other players were carried off the platform shoulder high. The *Western Mail* reporter wrote: "It was difficult to realise that the Bluebirds were not actually the League champions". They would never come as close again.

1923-24 First Division	P	W	D	L	F	A	Pts
1 Huddersfield	42	23	11	8	60	33	57
2 Cardiff	42	22	13	7	61	34	57
3 Sunderland	42	22	9	11	71	54	53
4 Bolton	42	18	14	10	68	34	50
5 Sheff United	42	19	12	11	69	49	50
6 Aston Villa	42	18	13	11	52	37	49
7 Everton	42	18	13	11	62	53	49
8 Blackburn	42	17	11	14	54	50	45
9 Newcastle	42	17	10	15	60	54	44
10 Notts County	42	14	14	14	44	49	42
11 Man City	42	15	12	15	54	71	42
12 Liverpool	42	15	11	16	49	48	41
13 West Ham	42	13	15	14	40	43	41
14 Birmingham	42	13	13	16	41	49	39
15 Tottenham	42	12	14	16	50	56	38
16 WBA	42	12	14	16	51	62	38
17 Burnley	42	12	12	18	55	60	36
18 Preston	42	12	10	20	52	67	34
19 Arsenal	42	12	9	21	40	63	33
20 Nottm Forest	42	10	12	20	42	64	32
21 Chelsea	42	9	14	19	31	53	32
22 Middlesbrough	42	7	8	27	37	60	22

So near and yet so far. Nowadays the Bluebirds would have been champions because they had scored one more goal than Huddersfield but in 1924 goal average, dividing "goals for" by "goals against", settled the issue.

Teams:

Cardiff City: Farquharson; Nelson, Blair; Wake, Keenor, Hardy; Davies, Gill, Jones, Clennell, Evans.

Birmingham City: Tremelling; Ashurst, Womack; Liddell, Cringen, Barton; Hayland, Crosbie, Bradford, Talin, Linden.

FA Cup Round Six: Wednesday 9 March 1927

Cardiff City (2) 3 Chelsea (1) 2

The 1926-27 season was an indifferent one for Cardiff City as far as the League was concerned and at one stage the club appeared to be likely candidates for relegation. Few people could have foreseen that the second half of the season would become the most glorious in City's history as the team mounted its challenge to win the FA Cup.

The Bluebirds' campaign began with a narrow 2-1 win against Aston Villa at Ninian Park in the third round. A trip to Darlington followed where the City struggled against the Third Division team, before emerging with an unconvincing 2-0 victory. Few expected the side to progress any further when the team was drawn away to Bolton Wanderers, the Cup holders. In front of a crowd of nearly 50,000, the game was marked by a number of controversial refereeing decisions but proved to be the turning point of the Bluebirds' season as they deservedly won 2-0.

Excitement was now building as Cardiff faced Chelsea from the Second Division at Stamford Bridge. On 5 March over 70,000 spectators witnessed a hard fought contest on a treacherous pitch. Though City dominated for long periods, the game

The programme for the replayed cup-tie with Chelsea shows both teams and also reviews the progress of Reading, the team City would meet in the semi-final.

ended in a scoreless draw but confidence was high that the replay at Ninian Park would carry the team into the semi-finals.

Attendances had fallen to a pathetic 8,000 at times that season owing to high unemployment, especially among the mining community, but somehow nearly 49,000 people found their way to Ninian Park for this replay. They saw an encounter packed with drama. After ten minutes **Sam Irving** scored after Len Davies's shot rebounded from the crossbar and 15 minutes later **Davies** added a second with a hard, low shot.

The visitors were far from finished and were awarded a penalty after Tommy Sloan had fouled Bob Turnbull. Farquharson stood poised at the back of the net as Andy Wilson prepared to take the penalty. As he was about to kick the ball, Farquharson sprang forward and smothered it on the six-yard line. Up to now this had been a legitimate ploy but, as other goalkeepers copied Farquharson's tactic, the present rule for taking penalties was introduced.

This was the penalty save that led to a change in the rules of football. Now a goalkeeper must stand on his line until the ball is kicked.

Seconds before half-time came another dramatic moment. **Priestley** hit a thundering cross shot which most people felt had gone wide of the upright. The referee, Mr. Pennington, first gave a goal kick before consulting a policeman behind the net. He confirmed that the ball had passed between the posts. Priestley's shot was so powerful that it had ripped away the pegs holding the net down.

As if there had not been enough excitement, Chelsea equalised soon after the interval. **Turnbull** scrambled the ball into the net from a free kick and City's prospects looked ominous when Curtis had to leave the field with a knee injury. He soon returned and, despite limping badly, continued to cause problems for the Chelsea defence. It was from his cross that Wilding foolishly handled with seven minutes remaining. It was the second penalty of the game but, unlike his Chelsea counterpart, **Hughie Ferguson** made no mistake.

As the game ended the crowd surged on to the pitch, perhaps feeling this was Cardiff's year. Reading were comfortably beaten in the semi-final and the Bluebirds were back at Wembley for their second final in three years. They had lost 1-0 to Sheffield United in 1925. This time the same team that conquered Chelsea went on to defeat Arsenal on St. George's Day, thus becoming the first side to take the FA Cup out of England. That 1-0 triumph has become legend but it was the stirring replay with Chelsea that was a crucial moment on the road to Wembley.

Tom Farquharson was the man of the match, if only for that brilliant penalty save. He arrived in South Wales after being involved in IRA activities, though these were of a non-violent nature. After playing in the Welsh League for Abertillery he joined

As Chelsea look for a late equaliser, Bob Turnbull's shot is saved by Farquharson. Jimmy Nelson is the player challenging Turnbull.

The same Cardiff City team that defeated Chelsea went on to win the FA Cup. Here they are shown in the positions they occupied in that team.

Cardiff in February 1922. He made 509 appearances for the club in the next 12 years and was undoubtedly the finest goalkeeper in the club's history.

Despite the heroics of the City team in 2008, this is still the Bluebirds' greatest moment as Fred Keenor collects the FA Cup at Wembley

The man who is still regarded as the greatest Bluebird of all was Fred Keenor and the cup victory against Arsenal was his proudest moment. Born in the Roath district of Cardiff, Fred signed for the City in 1912 and during the next 19 years he played 505 times for the club. His courage was never in doubt, as might be expected of a man who fought at the Somme and was twice wounded in World War I. Keenor was an inspiring captain with his will to win and his determined tackling. Among City fans he is still a folk hero and will always be remembered as the man who lifted the FA Cup on that great day in 1927.

Football League Division I: Saturday 1 September 1928

Cardiff City (4) 7 Burnley (0) 0

There was no sign of what a disastrous season was to follow for Cardiff City when a crowd of just over 20,000 gathered for this first home match. Before the game began the new Grangetown Stand was officially opened by the Lord Mayor, Alderman A.J. Howell, who cut a blue and white ribbon with a pair of silver scissors.

The pattern of the game was set in the first minute when a centre from Len Davies was headed home by **Hughie Ferguson**. For a time Burnley replied with some attractive football without looking likely to penetrate the City defence. The floodgates opened after a quarter of an hour as the Bluebirds scored three times in ten minutes. First Down held on to a free kick from Keenor but **Len Davies** followed up to bundle him into the net. Soon afterwards **Len Davies** took advantage of a misunderstanding between McCluggage and Down to score again. Down was having a miserable afternoon and, following some clever interplay between Thirlaway and Stan Davies, he could only parry a shot from **Ferguson** who netted the rebound to make it 4-0.

After the fireworks of the first half, the Burnley forwards showed the ability that had gained them a 7-2 victory at Newcastle a few days earlier and only the brilliance of Farquharson kept them at bay. The Bluebirds were content to hang on to their substantial lead and the crowd seemed happy to bask in the glorious sunshine. Then, midway through the half, the game once more exploded into life as **Ferguson** hit three more goals in quick succession. The first came from a Len Davies cross and soon afterwards Down was again at fault. He dropped the ball from a McLachlan centre and **Ferguson** gratefully accepted the gift. Stan Davies, who had an outstanding game, created the best goal of the day. Showing superb ball control he slipped a perfect pass

Ninian Park in 1930. The Grangetown Stand (right) could accommodate 18,000 fans and for many supporters was a favourite viewing point for the next 50 years.

Hughie Ferguson looks on as Len Davies shoulder charges the Burnley goalkeeper to score Cardiff's second goal.

to **Ferguson** who drove the ball home for his fifth and Cardiff's seventh goal of the afternoon.

In many ways it was a strange game in which Burnley played much better than the result suggested. Poor Down had a dreadful match and his errors gave a flattering appearance to the final score. However, *Citizen* believed Cardiff's victory was no fluke and prophesied: "I feel certain the City are bound to get a heavy crop of goals this season". He could not have been more wrong.

A 7-0 win is bound to inspire optimism in any team but Dick German's forecast in this cartoon was to prove well wide of the mark.

After scoring eight goals in their opening two matches, the Bluebirds could only muster another 35 in their remaining 40. They won only seven more games that season and, despite having the best defensive record in the First Division, they were relegated.

The team that had won the Cup two years earlier was now in the process of breaking up. Ernie Curtis moved to Birmingham in the 1927-28 season, though he returned to Cardiff for a short time in 1933. Watson and Sloan returned to Ireland and in 1930 Jimmy Nelson was transferred to Newcastle, where he captained their Cup winning team two years later. Fred Keenor moved to Crewe in 1931 where he played for another three years. Billy Hardy ended his long career with the City when he joined Bradford Park Avenue as coach in the summer of 1932. The saddest departure of all was that of Hughie Ferguson, the first Cardiff City player to score five goals in a match.

He came to Cardiff from Motherwell in November 1925 for £5,000, a large fee in those days. He repaid the club by scoring 87 goals in 131 appearances, including the winning goal in the 1927 Cup Final. At the end of the 1928-29 season Hughie was transferred to Dundee but, as he was suffering from a back injury, he could not repeat his earlier goal scoring feats. Dundee supporters began to barrack him and Ferguson,

The City team that played Burnley; Back row (left to right): Tommy Sloan, George McLachlan, Tom Farquharson, Stan Davies, Jack Jennings, Jimmy Nelson. Front row; Billy Thirlaway, Len Davies, Fred Keenor, Hughie Ferguson, Billy Hardy.

a sensitive man who had enjoyed hero worship at Cardiff, became increasingly depressed. After a training session, he committed suicide and was found dead next to a gas ring in Dundee's dressing room.

Hughie Ferguson, seen here with his wife, Jessie, was a Cardiff City legend but sadly he killed himself on 8 January 1930. He was just 32 years old.

Teams:

Cardiff City: Farquharson; Nelson, Jennings; Keenor, Sloan, Hardy; Thirlaway, Davies (S), Ferguson, Davies (L), Mclachlan.

Burnley: Down; McCluggage, Waterfield; Steel, Hill, Parkin; Bruton, Stage, Beel, Devine, Page.

A MISERABLE DECADE

Two years after their relegation from Division I, the Bluebirds sank into the Third Division. Their fall had been as meteoric as their rise. Amid the distress of mass unemployment and fears of war, crowds began to plummet and City's performances on the field reflected the misery of South Wales at that time. Only the successes of a very good Welsh team provided consolation for football lovers.

Football League Division III (South): Saturday 6 February 1932

Cardiff City (5) 9 Thames AFC (0) 2

The Thames club was formed in 1928 by a group of businessmen with the intention of making greater use of the West Ham Stadium, where the main activities were greyhound and speedway racing. The ground had a capacity of 120,000 but in December 1930 only 469 people were present in that vast arena to watch Thames play Luton Town, the lowest ever attendance in the League.

Before the match with Cardiff, Thames were bottom of Division III and even the presence of an ex-City favourite, Len Davies, was not enough to raise the crowd above 6,000. He was given a warm welcome as Thames took the field, wearing Welsh international jerseys borrowed from Len's collection.

CARTOON BY J. C. WALKER

LEN AIRS HIS INTERNATIONAL JERSEYS

WHAT'S BEEN AT 'EM, LEN — MOTHS?

NO, BLUEBIRDS!

NINIAN PARK

Every player in the Thames team with the exception of the goalkeeper turned out against Cardiff City at Ninian Park on Saturday clad in one of Len Davies's old International jerseys. It was Len's idea; he wanted to give the old jerseys an airing, and judging by the result of the game his scheme proved very successful.
(Result: Cardiff City, 9 goals, Thames, 2.)

As the Bluebirds ran up a record victory against Thames, J.C. Walker observes that Len Davies's old international shirts failed to bring his team any luck.

CITY SET THAMES ON FIRE!

ROBBINS' GREAT FEAT AT NINIAN PARK

3 GOALS IN 5 MINUTES!

Robbins was in great form, scoring five of the nine goals. Len Davies's only compensation was the fact that he scored one of his side's two goals.

Three goals in five minutes!

That was the great thrill that Robbins kept for Cardiff City supporters at Ninian Park this afternoon. This feat is the more amazing when it is remembered that Robbins was playing on the City's left wing!

Perhaps it was Len Davies' Welsh international jerseys that made the City "see red." Whatever the cause, it must be said that the City took advantage of their obvious superiority, and Thames were easily beaten by nine goals to two.

This is Cardiff City's best feat in English League football, and credit goes largely to the forwards, who snapped up every opportunity.

The Football Echo headlines pay tribute to Walter Robbins' memorable achievement in scoring five goals against Thames.

A goal by **McCambridge** in 90 seconds indicated the path the game was going to take but it was the performance of 21 year old **Walter Robbins** that proved to be the highlight of the match. He scored a hat trick in five minutes in the first half, though goalkeeping errors by Bailie helped him. To add to his woes, **Bailie** fumbled a corner from Emmerson into his own net to give City a 5-0 lead at the interval.

After **Keating** scored a sixth goal, Thames had their best spell of the match. First **McCarthy** scored a superb goal with a 25 yard shot which gave Farquharson no chance. Soon afterwards, to a great cheer, **Len Davies** scored a second to make the score 6-2. It was only a temporary respite and in the last ten minutes the Bluebirds added three more to their total, two of them from **Robbins** and the other from centre forward **Jones**.

The score flattered the Bluebirds and mistakes by Bailie, who had a nightmare match, contributed to the size of the Cardiff victory. This does not detract from the performance of Robbins who shared with Hughie Ferguson the club record for the most goals scored in a Football League match. His five goals were all the more remarkable as Walter was playing on the left wing.

Two months later Robbins was transferred to West Bromwich Albion for a substantial fee. Though he spent seven years with Albion, Walter never commanded a regular place and after World War II he returned to the Bluebirds as their trainer, sharing in their success of the post-war years.

The match against Thames remains a record League victory for Cardiff. The team was certainly entertaining that season as it scored 87 goals. Unfortunately it conceded 73 and eventually finished ninth in the League, its best position in the Third

Walter Robbins was undoubtedly the finest prospect in the City team at this time but the club's financial difficulties led to his sale. After leaving Cardiff he went on to win ten international caps for Wales.

Division before World War II. As for Thames, the team ended the season in bottom place and their directors decided to wind up the club just four years after it had been formed. The massive West Ham Stadium was demolished in 1972 and is now a housing estate.

Teams:
Cardiff City: Farquharson; Morris, Roberts; Galbraith, Harris, Ronan; Emmerson, Keating, Jones, McCambridge, Robbins.
Thames AFC: Bailie; Donnelly, Smith; Warner, Pritchard, Riddoch; Brown, McCarthy, Davies, Handley, Dimmock.

Football League Division III (South): Saturday 24 February 1934

Cardiff City (0) 1 Bristol Rovers (2) 5

The 1933-34 season had opened with some encouraging results for the Bluebirds but, since losing away to Bristol Rovers in early October, they had taken only six points from 19 matches. In view of these poor performances, attendances at some matches had fallen as low as 3,000. So a crowd of 8,000, swollen by a large contingent of Rovers' supporters, some of whom had made the journey by air, was regarded as a welcome improvement

Ernie Curtis was once more playing in Cardiff City colours after returning from Birmingham a few months earlier. Playing for the visitors was Jimmy McCambridge, the former City player, who was given a warm reception when the teams took the field. McCambridge scored 53 goals in 100 appearances for Cardiff, including a club record of 26 in the 1931-32 season. His transfer to Bristol Rovers, for whom he also scored heavily, was one of the many blunders made by the club at this time.

The black cat that wandered across the Cardiff goalmouth just before the game with Bristol Rovers was apparently one of their supporters. The Bluebirds certainly had no luck in this game.

The City team's lack of confidence was apparent in the opening stages as it took two excellent saves from Farquharson to prevent Bristol taking an early lead. The Bluebirds held out until a few minutes before half-time when a free kick, taken just outside Cardiff's penalty area, fell to **Havelock** who netted with a clever flick from close range. Almost at once **McNestry** was unchallenged as he set off on a run and, after beating Jenkins and Durkan, scored from a narrow angle.

Two down at half-time, it appeared likely that the Bluebirds would collapse in view of their recent form but after ten minutes a well taken corner by Marriott was headed home by **Eli Postin** to reduce the arrears. Soon afterwards Cardiff appeared to have a justified penalty claim when Pickering blatantly pushed Jim Henderson in the back.

It was against the run of play when **Jackson** dribbled through the Cardiff defence and scored a decisive third goal from a narrow angle. Rovers were now well on top and soon afterwards a good passing movement ended with an unmarked **McCambridge** driving in a shot that gave Farquharson no chance. Unquestionably Bristol were now the superior team, at times toying with the City players, and it was no surprise when **Havelock** headed a fifth goal five minutes from the end. By

Jim Henderson, City's centre forward, tries to win the ball in the Bristol Rovers' goalmouth but is well outnumbered in this heading duel

coincidence, earlier in the season, the other Bristol team had defeated Cardiff at Ninian Park by a similar score-line.

In a rather back-handed compliment the *Western Mail* reporter said: "City played about as well as they are capable of playing". The team tried to match Rovers' skill with honest endeavour but little went right for them and ultimately they were overwhelmed. Perhaps the margin of victory flattered Bristol Rovers and there were times in the game when the Bluebirds were on top.

The problem, as so often in this disastrous season, was a leaky defence which conceded 105 goals. Farquharson, now nearing the end of his career with Cardiff City,

Seven of this team played against Bristol Rovers. Back row (left to right); Leslie Adlam, Bob Calder, Tom Farquharson, George Russell, Eddie Jenkins, Eli Postin. Front row; Eddie Marcroft, Tom Maidment, Leslie Jones, Ernie Curtis, John Duthie, Alex Hutchinson.

	P	W	D	L	F	A	Pts
1 Norwich	42	25	11	6	88	49	61
2 Coventry	42	21	12	9	100	54	54
3 Reading	42	21	12	9	82	50	54
4 QPR	42	24	6	12	70	51	54
5 Charlton	42	22	8	12	83	56	52
6 Luton	42	21	10	11	83	61	52
7 Bristol Rovers	42	20	11	11	77	47	51
8 Swindon	42	17	11	14	64	68	45
9 Exeter	42	16	11	15	68	57	43
10 Brighton	42	15	13	14	68	60	43
11 Clapton Orient	42	16	10	16	75	69	42
12 Crystal Palace	42	16	9	17	71	67	41
13 Northampton	42	14	12	16	71	78	40
14 Aldershot	42	13	12	17	52	71	38
15 Watford	42	15	7	20	71	63	37
16 Southend	42	12	10	20	51	74	34
17 Gillingham	42	11	11	20	75	96	33
18 Newport	42	8	17	17	49	70	33
19 Bristol City	42	10	13	19	58	85	33
20 Torquay	42	13	7	22	53	93	33
21 Bournemouth	42	9	9	24	60	102	27
22 Cardiff	42	9	6	27	57	105	24

The 1933-34 Third Division table tells the story of City's sad decline. Ten years earlier the Bluebirds had narrowly missed becoming the Football League Champions.

was still a superb goalkeeper but inexperienced young players such as Jack Durkan and Ernest Lewis were clearly out of their depth. Nine players from the team that played Rovers were not retained at the end of the season. Their departure made little difference as City continued to struggle at the lower end of the Third Division.

The game with Bristol Rovers was one of the most depressing days of the worst year in Cardiff City's history. A few months later the Bluebirds had to face the humiliation of seeking re-election to the Football League. While there was never any doubt that they would be re-admitted, it was a bitter pill to swallow for the club that only seven years ago had won the Cup.

Teams:

Cardiff City: Farquharson; Calder, Durkan; Lewis (E), Jenkins, Molloy; Marcroft, Postin, Henderson, Curtis, Hutchinson.

Bristol Rovers: Preedy; Pickering, Donald; Wallington, McLean, Ayres; McNestry, McKay, Havelock, McCambridge, Jackson.

FA Cup Round Three: Saturday 16 January 1937

Cardiff City (0) 1 Grimsby Town (3) 3

Billy Bassett was the linch-pin of the City defence between 1934 and 1939. His injury in the game with Grimsby was a major blow to Cardiff's hopes against the First Division team.

Little went right for the Bluebirds in those miserable days of the 1930s and this cup-tie turned out to be one of the darkest moments in that era. The game appeared to have the ingredients for an exciting afternoon and the crowd of 36,000 was the largest seen at Ninian Park for many years. Grimsby were a mid-table team in Division I and began the game as favourites but, though City were in the lower reaches of the Third Division, the advantage of playing at home suggested there was the chance of a giant killing performance.

Indeed, in the opening minutes the Bluebirds matched their opponents with an exhilarating display of attacking football. Reg Pugh and Eugene Melaniphy both came close to scoring before the game was ruined by two accidents. Vincent, the Grimsby fullback, was injured after 10 minutes and spent the rest of the game playing on the wing. Almost immediately City's centre half Billy Bassett suffered a recurrence of a groin injury which had kept him out of action for a month. He returned to play on the left wing but was no more than a passenger for the rest of the game.

Bassett's hard tackling was vital to the Bluebirds in a game such as this and, though each side was now playing with only ten fit men, his injury proved to be a decisive blow for Cardiff's hopes. While Bassett was off the field Grimsby scored twice against the run of play. **Lewis** headed the first goal as the referee ignored his linesman's flag for offside. Even more bizarre was the second after 20 minutes. **Craven** appeared to be so obviously offside that the City defenders stopped playing and the Grimsby player strolled through the defence for an easy goal. The game was over by half-time when **Glover** was unmarked and easily beat George Poland with a low shot.

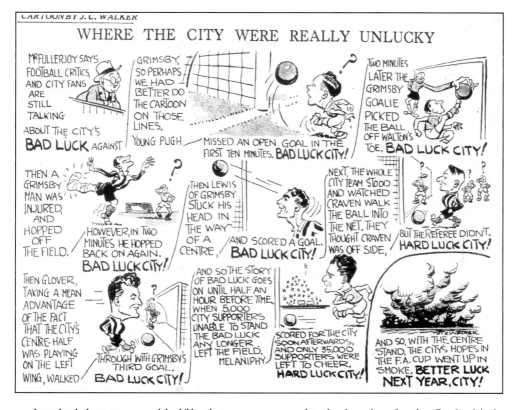

The cartoon sums up a thoroughly miserable weekend for the Bluebirds. Losing a cup-tie was bad enough but losing the Grandstand was an even greater blow.

In a lack lustre second half both teams appeared to be longing for the final whistle though **Melaniphy** was able to score a consolation goal for Cardiff near the end. By this time the ground was half empty and, while the final score flattered Grimsby, those still present were happy to hear the final whistle as one of the dullest cup-ties ever seen at Ninian Park came to an end.

The real drama surrounding this match was still to come. At 3.45 a.m. the following Monday, a policeman discovered fire erupting from the Grandstand. Fanned by a strong wind, flames burst through the roof of the stand and in less than an hour only a skeleton of twisted girders remained. The corrugated roof of the Canton Stand was red hot from the heat but firemen made certain the fire did not spread to

Fire destroyed the Grandstand after the game with Grimsby. The blaze was so fierce that it could be seen as far away as the city centre

this area. However, the offices and the dressing rooms with the players' kit were completely destroyed. Trixie, the black cat who had been City's mascot in the 1927 Cup Final, was rescued by firemen, though her fur was badly singed. Sadly Jack, the club's watchdog, was less fortunate and he perished in the flames.

The cause of the fire was probably an attempted burglary to seize the takings from Saturday's match. A petrol can was found near the safe in the office and there were indications that someone had tampered with it. In fact the safe was empty as the gate receipts of £2,000 had been removed from the ground immediately after the match.

Temporary changing rooms were erected behind the Canton Stand until a new structure was built. Constructed in steel and concrete, it now forms the centre part of the present Grandstand. It could hold 1,500 spectators and was adequate for the club's needs at that time.

This view of Ninian Park shows the new Grandstand that was opened in 1938. Not until 1973 were two new wings added so that the stand once more ran the length of the pitch.

Teams:
Cardiff City: Poland; Granville, Mellor; Nicholson, Bassett, Godfrey; Pugh, Pinxton, Melaniphy, Talbot, Walton.
Grimsby Town: Tweedy; Vincent, Kelly; Hall, Hodgson, Buck; Dyson, Bestall, Craven, Lewis.

Home International Championship:
Saturday 22 October 1938

Wales (2) 4 England (2) 2

Before the days of saturation television coverage, international matches were an opportunity to see the great stars of British football and perhaps look back with nostalgia to the days when the City could welcome these players on a regular basis. The Welsh team had won the Home Championship three times in the last six years but, as they took the field for this match, they were regarded as the underdogs.

Two talented sides lined up for the international between Wales and England in October 1938. Sadly Roy John of Swansea was the only player representing a Welsh Club

The England team was considered to be their best for many years and some English critics patronisingly suggested the game would be a useful preparation for their encounter the following week against the Rest of Europe. Two players in the side would become household names. Stanley Matthews, the "Wizard of dribble", whose career would span more than 30 years, was on the right wing and Tommy Lawton, one of the finest centre-forwards the game has seen, was making his first appearance for his country. The duel between Lawton and his Everton clubmate, Tommy Jones, was expected to be one of the highlights of the afternoon. So was the skilful artistry of Bryn Jones, for whom Arsenal had recently paid a record transfer fee of £14,000.

By the time of the kick-off there were well over 50,000 people in the ground and, in a dramatic opening, they saw Wales take the lead after only five minutes. Leslie Jones drew centre half Young out of position and slipped the ball to **Dai Astley** who hit a scorching drive past Woodley.

These smiling faces were part of the huge crowd, watching the match with England. As Cardiff City fans had little to cheer about in the 1930s, international matches were a welcome relief.

It was against the run of play when England equalised after half an hour. In a goal mouth scramble the ball was kicked against the arm of a Welsh player and rather harshly the referee awarded a penalty. **Lawton** made no mistake with the kick. In this pulsating first half, Wales quickly regained the lead in a rather lucky fashion. **Hopkins** challenged Woodley who tried to fist the ball away but only succeeded in turning it into his own net. Almost at once, it was England's turn to have a slice of luck. In his later career **Stan Matthews** was rarely a goal scorer but on this occasion he wandered into a central position and, as he hit the ball, Roy John allowed the ball to bounce over his arm and England were once again level.

In the first half the England team had played a careful passing game, reminiscent of continental sides, while the Welsh, playing with their traditional fervour, were more direct in their approach. After the interval the English players raised the tempo of their game with slick passing and fast, attacking football. Roy John was kept busy as he made several fine saves to keep Wales in the game.

It was against the run of play when Astley, who was having a superb match, sent a through ball to **Bryn Jones** who made no mistake to restore the Welsh lead. Fittingly

A hectic moment around the Welsh goal as Roy John and Tommy Jones are challenged by an England forward for the ball.

it was Astley who made the game safe with the best goal of the match. In a three man move, Bryn Jones sent a wide pass to Cumner who slipped the ball to **Astley**. He swept past Young as though he did not exist and coolly slid the ball past Woodley.

Wales had confounded their critics, not for the first time, and fully deserved to win what had been a magnificent game. Dai Astley, whose ball control, positional play and lethal finishing contributed so much to the Welsh success, was undoubtedly the best player on the field. He was a last minute replacement for Pat Glover and had not played for Wales for three years. Few men have made a more spectacular comeback in the Welsh jersey.

Throughout the 1930s Wales were the strongest side of the home nations and might have achieved even greater success if English clubs had always been prepared to release their players. British teams did not participate in the World Cup at that time but, if they had, it is interesting to speculate how this Welsh team might have fared in the competition.

The FOOTBALL ASSOCIATION of WALES Ltd.

INTERNATIONAL FOOTBALL MATCH

NINIAN PARK CARDIFF.

• OFFICIAL • PROGRAMME
TWOPENCE •

SATURDAY, October 22, 1938
KICK-OFF 3.15

ENGLAND v WALES

HANCOCKS
Amber Ale
FOURPENCE A BOTTLE
a brew that is making history

The cover of the programme for the 1938 international. The programmes were not so elaborate in those days but, on the other hand, they cost less than 1p in today's money.

Football League Division III (South): Saturday 31 December 1938

Cardiff City (0) 1 Newport County (1) 2

Towards the end of the 1930s the prospects for Cardiff City began to look a little brighter. Attendances were rising as the economic depression began to ease and results too showed an improvement. The last match of 1938 attracted a crowd of nearly 40,000 and, on the day, only Newcastle had a bigger attendance in the whole of the Football League. With County topping the Third Division table and enjoying the most successful season in their history, there was no shortage of vocal support from Gwent for this derby game.

The programme for the match between City and Newport County in 1938. The sketch is inaccurate as it shows the old Grandstand which had been burnt down the previous year.

The County players immediately settled into their stride and showed why they were League leaders. After six minutes **Arthur Hydes** fastened on to a pass from Derrick and scored with a brilliant shot. Newport's positional play and better teamwork continued to give them the edge though, midway through the half, City managed to exert some pressure without looking particularly dangerous. Instead Hydes might have increased County's lead but Fielding kept Cardiff in the game with a brilliant save.

The Bluebirds lacked the cohesion of the County team but their determination led to an equaliser ten minutes after the restart. McCaughey began the move and **Ritchie Smith** forced his way through the Newport defence to beat the advancing Ferguson. For the first time in the game City appeared the more likely team to score but County weathered the storm and, with 15 minutes remaining, regained the lead. There was an element of luck about the goal as Kelso was obstructed and was unable to stop Duggan's pass to Hydes. From his centre **Carr** scored the winner with a diving header. It was a fair result for, while the Bluebirds had an equal share of possession, they were far more disjointed in their approach.

It was Newport's day and in May the team was able to celebrate a deserved promotion to Division II. Sadly, the players who had earned it were only able to play three matches the following season before World War II brought proceedings to an end. The team after the war was not strong enough to retain its hard won status and in 1947 County returned to the Third Division. Since that time of course they have fallen out of the Football League and are still a long way from returning.

Arthur Hydes gives Newport the lead despite the efforts of Jimmy Kelso (left) and Bill Bassett to stop him.

Mr. Fullerjoy was J.C. Walker's creation. In this cartoon he makes some humorous observations about the Bluebirds' performance against Newport.

City ended this last full season before the war in 13th place. The match against Newport was followed by a cup-tie when another large crowd witnessed a giant killing act as Cardiff beat Charlton from the First Division. Matters were improving but the club was not occupying a position worthy of a city the size of Cardiff. Significantly in April 1939 two important decisions were made for the club's future. Herbert Merrett was appointed as chairman and Cyril Spiers joined the club as secretary-manager from Wolverhampton's training staff. With Merrett's support, Spiers began the process of leading Cardiff City back to better times.

Teams:
Cardiff City: Fielding; Ballsom, Kelso; McCaughey, Bassett Main; Rhodes, Walton, Collins, Egan, Smith.
Newport County: Ferguson; Roberts, Richards; Lawrence, Low, Brinton; Duggan, Hydes, Derrick, Wood, Carr.

Football League Division III (South): 2 September 1939

Cardiff City (1) 2 Notts County (1) 4

The programme for 2 September 1939 shows how the teams lined up for the last League match at Ninian Park before the outbreak of World War II.

This match was played in what was almost certainly the most unreal atmosphere ever experienced at Ninian Park. The previous day Hitler had invaded Poland and the British Government presented Germany with an ultimatum that unless her troops were withdrawn, Britain would go to war. The cricket season had already come to an abrupt end but the authorities agreed that football fixtures should continue until war was actually declared.

The gravity of the international situation was indicated by the number of spectators at matches on that last Saturday before hostilities began. At most games attendances fell below 10,000 and Cardiff's crowd of 20,000, many of them in military uniform, was among the highest of the day. Perhaps the desire to escape for a few hours from the grim shadow over-hanging the nation drew people to Ninian Park, but Cardiff's bright start to the

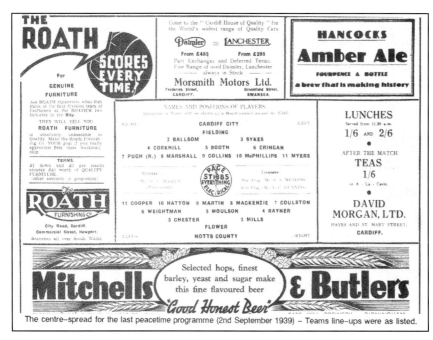

The centre-spread for the last peacetime programme (2nd September 1939) - Teams line-ups were as listed.

season, the best for several years, had also aroused interest. The Bluebirds had won their first two away games at Norwich and Swindon and this was their first home match of the season.

The "All Clear" at Ninian Park

Flower punches clear in a City attack on the Notts County goal as Moulson (number 5) looks on. This was the first season in which players could be identified by numbers.

Notts County controlled the match in the early stages and took the lead after 15 minutes through **Jim McKenzie**, a former City player. Within five minutes **Jimmy Collins** equalised for the Bluebirds but, though they missed chances to take the lead before half-time, their limitations were shown after the interval as Notts took control.

J.C. Walker chose a topical theme for this cartoon. The blitzing of Southampton and Norwich are a reference to Newport's and Cardiff's victories the previous Saturday.

The County players were faster, distributed the ball better, and displayed much superior cohesion as a team. Martin should have scored when he shot wide with only Bill Fielding to beat. It was only a temporary respite, and on the hour mark **Hatton** restored County's lead with a fine individual goal. Notts were now well on top and it was no surprise when Coulston broke away on the right and, as Fielding came out to meet him, he passed the ball to **Martin** who stroked the ball into an empty net. From a free kick on the edge of the penalty area, **Collins** was able to fire the ball through a crowd of players to reduce the arrears. The visitors soon regained their two goal advantage when **Martin** collected a cross from the left to hammer the ball into the net.

As the spectators drifted away, most of them realised they had seen their last Football League match for many years. On Sunday war was declared and on Monday players' contracts were terminated by all League clubs. Places of entertainment were closed on Government orders because of the fear that air raids could cause enormous casualties at theatres, cinemas or sporting venues.

Later, realising that entertainment was important to raise the morale of the people,

CARTOON   By J. C. WALKER

THE WELSH BOMBERS

rules were relaxed. Football grounds were re-opened with a reduced capacity and leagues were formed on a regional basis. Clubs were allowed to enlist "guest" players who were serving in the armed forces in their area. Among the guests used by Cardiff in the early years of the war, were Raich Carter and Bill Shankly.

None of those who played against Notts County in that last pre-war fixture figured in City's plans when hostilities ended. Billy Baker, who played a few games for the club before the war, suffered brutal treatment from the Japanese as a prisoner of war but went on to become one of the stalwarts of that famous post-war team. Another talented young player on the City's books in 1939 was Billy James. He too fell into Japanese hands but, unlike Baker, he never recovered from his ordeal and failing eyesight forced him to retire in 1947.

Football is pushed into the background as the grim headlines in the Football Echo prepare the nation for war.

When League football resumed after the war, the fixture list was the same as that of 1939. The City's results of those last pre-war days were all reversed in 1946 and, after losing to Norwich and Swindon, the Bluebirds notched their first victory against Notts County in what would prove to be a memorable season.

REVIVAL AFTER WORD WAR II

When hostilities ended, Cardiff City reaped the benefit of Cyril Spiers' policy of relying on local talent rather than guest players during the war years. The team that won promotion to the Second Division in 1947 is still regarded as one of the finest to wear the City colours and, five years later, the team was back in Division I, a rise comparable with that after the First World War

Friendly Match: Saturday 17 November 1945

Cardiff City (0) 1 Moscow Dynamo (3) 10

The visit of the famous Moscow Dynamo team to Britain was one of the highlights of the 1945-46 season. Following Dynamo's first match against Chelsea, when an 85,000 crowd packed into Stamford Bridge to witness a 3-3 draw, the Russians travelled to Cardiff for their next engagement. The game was really an after thought because Dynamo wanted to be involved in a Saturday fixture, and the Bluebirds were one of the few teams available to play on that day.

There was tremendous excitement as the Russians arrived in Cardiff two days before the match. No-one knew much about them and only later did it emerge that the team was drawn from the Soviet security forces, the KGB. In 1945 there was still great admiration for the heroism displayed by the Russians during the war and the Lord Mayor gave them a civic reception. Wherever they went, they were given a warm welcome. Visits to the National Museum, the Docks and a local coal mine were organised and they were entertained by a Welsh choir. Stand tickets for the game were sold out on the day they were issued and a huge crowd was anticipated. In fact fears of

NEWS OF THE WORLD

BRITAIN'S GREATEST NEWSPAPER.

Moscow Dynamo v. Cardiff City

Read the SPECIAL REPORT IN TO-MORROW'S "NEWS OF THE WORLD."

Net Sale Exceeds 4,000,000 Copies per Issue.

SPORT IS NATIONALISED IN RUSSIA.

Before the war, Russia spent 600,000,000 roubles on sport for the people. There are now 650 stadiums, ranging from the great Dynamo Stadium in Moscow—which is larger than Wembley—to moderately sized ones. The number of sports grounds was last given as 7,000. Sixteen years ago the All-Union Council of Physical Culture was set up. This is the supreme authority in the U.S.S.R. on all sports.

While there is no International competition, as yet, it is difficult to assess standards, especially in the realm of Association football, which has steadily gained in popularity during the past 15 years.

One difficulty about International contests is the fact that the Russian soccer season starts just as ours in Britain enters the close season.

All sport in Russia is looked upon primarily from the point of view of the player and not the spectator.

Favourite Russian sport still remains chess, with draughts not far behind.

If the U.S.S.R. enter a full team at the next Olympic games, she will certainly score many successes.

TO OUR CIVILIAN COMMANDOS.

We kindly entreat the enthusiasts to keep their feet on the ground this afternoon. All Stand roofs and hoardings are unsafe as sight-seeing venues. Be good lads this time. Hospitals are not looking for customers. Prevent a minor or major disaster by paying heed to this well-meant advice.

Spectators are asked to keep off the field of play. Nark it.

Take it easy after the game. Don't rush the exits. A steady and orderly retreat out of the ground will be beneficial to all. Thank you!

For those who knew little about sport in Russia, the programme for the match with Moscow Dynamo attempted to enlighten them.

Fred Stansfield accepts a bouquet of flowers from the Dynamo captain. The Russians were presented with miniature silver plated miners' lamps.

crowd congestion, such as that which had been experienced at Chelsea, kept the attendance down to a modest 31,000.

Cyril Spiers, who had seen the game at Chelsea, believed Dynamo, with its "spectacular attack and a stonewall defence", to be the best foreign team ever to visit Britain. The Russians had shown at Chelsea what a good side they were but few were prepared for the one-sided contest that followed at Cardiff. They sprang their first surprise when they came out 30 minutes before the kick-off with half a dozen footballs and began their warm up procedures. Today this practice is common but then it was unusual. Before the game began the national anthems were played and both sides were introduced to the Soviet ambassador and the Lord Mayor.

For a while City matched their illustrious opponents but after seven minutes a quickly taken free kick found **Bobrov** unmarked in front of goal, and he opened the

McLoughlin, the City goalkeeper, makes a valiant attempt to keep the ball out of the net but it is yet another clinical finish by the Russian team.

scoring with a header. Two minutes later the difference in class between the teams was underlined when **Beskov** fastened on to a beautiful through ball to score with a fast, low drive into the corner of the net. At this stage the Bluebirds were still in the game but their attacks broke down against solid defending and the brilliance of Dynamo goalkeeper, "Tiger" Khomich. Any chance of making a game of it ended as the Russians switched from defence to lightning attack for **Archangelski** to score a third goal

Three nil at half-time was almost respectable but the second half turned into a rout as Dynamo added seven more goals. **Archangelski** took his personal tally to four and both **Bobrov** and **Beskov** completed hat tricks. City did have their moments and some spectacular handling by Khomich, including a penalty save from Terry Wood, provided abiding memories for the crowd. The biggest cheer of the afternoon came when **Beriah Moore** scored for Cardiff between Dynamo's eighth and ninth goals.

The Russians were a revelation with their skilful interchanging of positions and the speed at which they played. It must be remembered that Cardiff were up against a team which was much fitter and had been carefully preparing for this tour. Most of the City players were still involved in war work and had to fit in their training whenever they could. Roy Clarke, for instance, was a Bevin boy. Nor was this Cardiff's best team as players such as Billy Rees and Alf Sherwood were not available.

The Dynamo players completed their tour with a victory at Arsenal and a draw at Rangers and returned home to be made "Heroes of the Soviet Union". As for the Cardiff City players, they soon shrugged off this freak result as the club prepared for a return to League football and one of the most successful seasons in its history.

J.C. Walker takes a wry look at City's afternoon against Moscow Dynamo but it must be remembered that it was a makeshift Cardiff team selected for this match.

Teams:

Cardiff City: Mcloughlin; Lever, Raybould; Hollyman, Stansfield, Lester; Moore, Carless, Gibson, Wood, Clarke.

Moscow Dynamo: Khomich; Radikorsky, Stankevich; Blinkov, Semichastny, Soloviev (L); Archangelsky, Kartsev, Beskov, Bobrov, Soloviev (S).

Football League Division III (South):
Monday 7 April 1947

The City team of 1946-47. Back row Left to right); Ken Hollyman, Bob Allison (trainer), Stan Richards, Dan Canning, Glyn Williams, Billy Rees, Bryn Allen, Roy Clarke. Middle row; Colin Gibson, Arthur Lever, Fred Stansfield, Alf Sherwood, George Wardle. Front row; Billy Baker, Bernard Ross.

Cardiff City (0) 1 Bristol City (1) 1

The Football League reverted to its traditional programme for the 1946-47 season and it proved to be among the most memorable in the club's history. In June 1946 Cyril Spiers resigned as manager after a dispute over his contract and his successor, Billy McCandless, was lucky enough to inherit one of the finest sides ever to represent Cardiff City. After three defeats in their opening six matches, the team embarked on a fantastic run in which they won 19 and drew two of the next 21 games. Amazingly, the Bluebirds were able to field virtually an unchanged team week after week. Most of these players had been signed by Spiers and ten of them were Welsh. Colin Gibson was the only Englishman in the side.

Attendances at all sporting events reached unprecedented levels after World War II. The City team attracted large crowds wherever they played but the attendance for the game with Bristol City reached 51,656, a record for a Third Division match. As all roads led to Ninian Park, one of their supporters said: "Half of Bristol is here already and the other half is on its way".

For months Cardiff seemed to have an unassailable lead at the top of the table but recently Queens Park Rangers had been edging closer as the Bluebirds showed signs of faltering. The Robins had inflicted a 2-1 defeat on the City at Ashton Gate on Good Friday and were hoping to cause further damage to Cardiff's promotion prospects in this game.

From the kick-off, the Bluebirds appeared jittery and the defence in particular made uncharacteristic errors. Lever, Stansfield and even Sherwood were all guilty of creating extra pressure by slicing their clearances and it was no surprise when Bristol went ahead after 15 minutes. **Williams (S)** took advantage of hesitancy among the City defenders to fire the ball past Canning. The visitors continued to look the more dangerous team and, though the Cardiff forwards created a few

Alf Sherwood (right) moves in to tackle Don Clark, Bristol City's leading scorer and father of Brian Clark, who signed for Cardiff in the late 1960s.

chances, over eagerness and sound handling by goalkeeper Ferguson kept them out.

After the interval, as the home side stepped up the pressure, Richards and Allen went close but the Robins' defence held firm and Ferguson in particular continued to frustrate them. The Bluebirds had not lost a home match all season but, as the clock ticked away, it appeared they were about to receive a hammer blow to their promotion hopes.

With almost the entire Bristol team in their own goalmouth, only ten minutes remained when Allen split their defence with a perfect pass to **Richards**. He advanced a few yards and, to the relief of the home supporters, beat Ferguson from close range. In the dying minutes Cardiff might have snatched the winner when Roy Clarke hit the post but the gallant Ferguson ensured that Bristol City would be the only team Cardiff failed to defeat that season.

Stan Richards, Cardiff's record breaking scorer. City fans used to sing, "Open the score, Richards", an adaptation of a popular song at the time.

Stan Richards was one of the last signings to be made by Cyril Spiers. He became a great favourite among City fans and his equaliser against Bristol City was his 27th goal of the season, a new club record. He went on to score 30 before the season was over, a record that stood until 2003 when it was surpassed by Robert Earnshaw.

The excitement was too much for one spectator who was perched on the roof of the Grangetown Stand. Sliding down to the front to get a better view, he fell on top of four unfortunate fans who cushioned his fall but sustained injuries themselves. The hole in the roof remained for some time as a warning to any other foolhardy spectator.

After the dreadful winter of 1947 the football season was extended into June when the Bluebirds were crowned champions of the Third Division South. It was the first championship the club had won and in doing so, the team had won 30 of their 42 matches, scoring 93 goals in the process while conceding only 30.

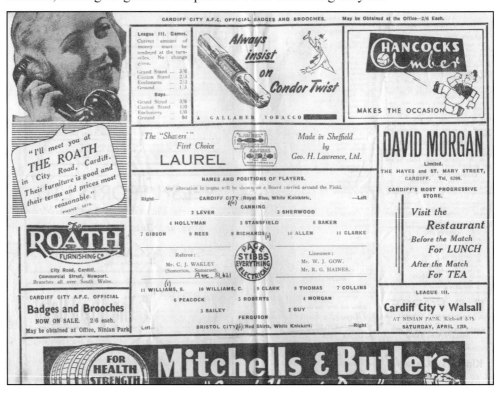

The teams for the Bristol City match. Charlie Hill was a late replacement for Billy Rees but, otherwise, the Bluebirds' line-up was that considered by many to be one of the best ever to represent the club.

Football League Division II:
Saturday 27 August 1949

Cardiff City (0) 1 Swansea Town (0) 0

The first encounter for 19 years between the two great Welsh rivals aroused eager anticipation and Welshmen travelled from all over Britain to see the game. Many were to be disappointed as the match was an all-ticket affair and the official attendance of 57,510 was a new ground record. Swansea had been relegated in the 1946-47 season when Cardiff were promoted but now the Swans were back in Division II. Though

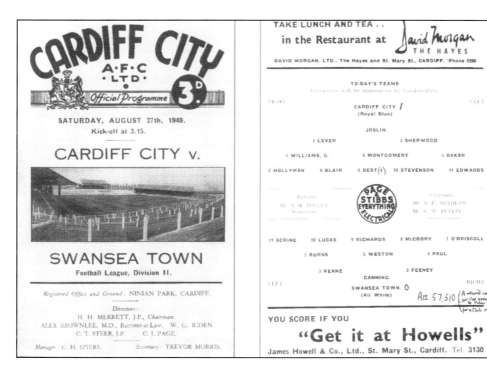

The programme for the first post-war contest between the Bluebirds and the Swans. The view of the ground at that time is taken from the popular bank.

there was plenty of banter there was no crowd trouble, and the fact that the Chief Constables of Cardiff and Swansea were present was mere coincidence.

The teams came out to a great reception with a special cheer reserved for two Swansea players in particular. Goalkeeper Dan Canning was in the stand because of an injury but both he and Stan Richards had been heroes of Cardiff's promotion campaign three years earlier. Also in the Swans' line-up was Roy Paul, one of the finest right-halves to represent Wales. In 1956 he would become the first Welshman since Fred Keenor to receive the FA Cup, when he captained Manchester City in their victory over Birmingham.

Phil Joslin comes out to challenge Jack O'Driscoll as Swansea's Frank Scrine looks on. Partially hidden in the picture are Billy Baker and "Buller" Lever.

On a beautiful, sunny afternoon conditions were ideal for football but, like most local derbies, there was a tension that prevented both teams from playing to their potential. O'Driscoll appeared to have scored for Swansea from a free kick but Referee Tolley, who had sent three players off the last time he had handled a Swansea game, disallowed it and insisted the kick must be retaken.

Swansea had the better chances and Phil Joslin was forced to make several fine saves, but the best chance of the first half fell to George Edwards whose powerful shot was cleared off the line by Jim Feeney. A head injury to Rory Keane reduced Swansea to ten men for a time though he soon returned with his head swathed in bandages. A scrappy first half ended with the score sheet blank.

After the restart Keane was moved to the left wing and the Swans were forced to reshuffle their team. Though the game continued to be fiercely fought, it never became over physical. Just when it appeared neither side would ever score, Weston miskicked his clearance and the ball fell to Glyn Williams. He hit the ball first time and it was deflected to **Tommy Best** who made no mistake to score the only goal of the match.

Swansea's goalkeeper, Parry, wins this duel with Best as they both go for a high ball. Best was a popular figure among City supporters in an era when there were few black players in League football.

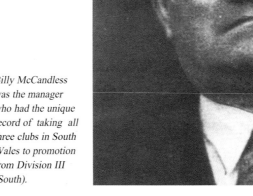

Billy McCandless was the manager who had the unique record of taking all three clubs in South Wales to promotion from Division III (South).

There was half an hour left for play and it was the most exciting period of the match as both sides created chances. Cardiff just about deserved to win, though the injury to Keane disrupted the Swansea team. Defences were generally on top throughout the game with Roy Paul and Billy Lucas outstanding for Swansea. For Cardiff, Joslin, a goalkeeper who may not have specialised in spectacular saves but rarely gave away silly goals, showed his usual coolness under pressure.

After the match there was a ceremony in the boardroom when Billy McCandless, the Swansea manager, was presented with a gold watch on behalf of the three clubs from South Wales. Swansea's promotion the previous season followed a similar achievement with Newport in 1939 and Cardiff in 1947. McCandless attributed his success to three boards of directors who never interfered with his team selection. City full back, Arthur Lever, paid him this tribute: "He knew how to get the best out of players, made sure the training staff got us fit, picked the side and then let us get on with it". He remained manager of Swansea until his death in 1955 at the age of 61.

The Cardiff fans were happy to see their side win this first derby between the teams since World War II but the Swans had their revenge on Christmas Eve, when the return game was played at the Vetch Field. In their best display of the season, they overran Cardiff to record a 5-1 victory. I was among the City supporters whose Christmas was spoilt that year.

Football League Division II: Saturday 5 January 1952

Cardiff City (1) 2 Doncaster Rovers (1) 1

Before this game the Bluebirds were lying third in Division II and were strong contenders for promotion. Doncaster, though they had beaten Cardiff earlier in the season, were in the lower reaches of the division and did not appear likely to offer a serious obstacle to the City's progress.

Cardiff dominated from the outset. In the first minute Mike Tiddy fired in a tremendous shot which Hardwick could not hold. Fortunately for the Doncaster keeper, the ball stuck on his line and he was able to gather it at the second attempt. Cardiff continued to dominate as Sullivan tried a shot from 20 yards that hit the post and a minute later Blair's header struck the crossbar. It seemed only a matter of time before Cardiff scored in spite of desperate measures, most of them illegal, from the Doncaster defenders.

The teams for the game between Cardiff and Doncaster Rovers. The game was to be one of the toughest the Bluebirds faced in their quest for promotion.

City's "Bandaged Hero" was the headline in the Football Echo when the City defeated Doncaster. The photograph shows Sherwood outwitting the Doncaster defence to score the winner.

Then, after half an hour, Alf Sherwood was forced to leave the field. He had received an injury above his eye in the match with Swansea on Christmas Day and only recently had the stitches been removed. In a clash with the Doncaster right winger, Calverley, the wound re-opened and for ten minutes the Bluebirds played with ten men. No substitutes were allowed in those days and the result of this match might have been different if Sherwood had been replaced.

Hardwick fists the ball away as Wilf Grant tries to head towards the Doncaster goal. George Edwards is the on-looking City player.

As it was, to great cheers, he re-appeared with his forehead heavily bandaged. Unfortunately, while he was waiting for the referee's permission to rejoin the game, Doncaster took the lead as **Harrison** scrambled the ball into the net from close range. With Cardiff's prospects looking gloomy, Alf took up a position on the right wing where he had once played in a schoolboy international. Just on the stroke of half-time a cross from Blair beat Hardwick and **Sherwood,** unmarked and standing almost on the goal line, netted the equaliser

Ten minutes after the interval the story book ending was completed. The Doncaster defenders had still not learnt that it was a mistake to give Alf too much room. This time it was a centre from Edwards that found **Sherwood** evading Hardwick and left-back Graham before coolly placing the ball in an empty net.

There were no more goals though Sherwood almost scored a hat-trick with a shot that just swerved past the post. Throughout the game, referee Barnes had given the City players little protection and Montgomery, Tiddy and Glyn Williams were all left limping after bruising tackles from the Doncaster defenders. However, the Bluebirds held on to their lead and, as Sheffield Wednesday, the eventual champions, and Birmingham both lost, the City returned to the top of the table. It remained a roller coaster ride for the rest of the season but the two points gained in this hard fought contest were to be vital in May.

Alf Sherwood takes the ball from Tom Finney with a perfect sliding tackle in an international match at Ninian Park in October 1951.

Alf Sherwood is still remembered as the finest full-back to play for Cardiff City. His duels with those two great England wingers, Stanley Matthews and Tom Finney, were legendary and Matthews said, "He was a fine and fair tackler, one of the best I came up against". Perhaps his greatest assets lay with his powers of recovery. Wingers would think they were past him only to discover he was still barring the way. He was also the best exponent of the sliding tackle in his era. It was a tackle that could be very dangerous if it was mistimed. Alf's timing was perfect and never once in his career was he sent off or booked.

Sherwood had shown not only a courageous spirit but also his versatility as a player. In those days full-backs rarely ventured into attacking positions. They were expected to defend and mark the opposing winger but, on that winter afternoon Sherwood showed he was the complete footballer who could play in virtually any position. Indeed he was a capable goalkeeper when the need arose and in April 1954 he condemned Liverpool to relegation from Division I when he saved a penalty kick from Billy Liddell. His value in today's transfer market would be enormous.

Football League Division II: Saturday 3 May 1952

Cardiff City (2) 3 Leeds United (0) 1

On the first Saturday in May the football season had ended for most clubs and this would be the last time any league matches would be played on the same day as the Cup Final. In that game Newcastle United defeated Arsenal 1-0 but few people in Cardiff were unduly interested in that result. City supporters had their minds on the match with Leeds United in which victory for Cardiff would see the return of First Division football to Wales.

Two weeks earlier, the Bluebirds' chances of promotion appeared to be remote. Before playing at Luton on 20 April they were five points behind Birmingham City with only four games to go. Throughout the season their away form had been indifferent and, with 20 minutes to go, they were losing 2-1. Then the City manager, Cyril Spiers, heard that Birmingham were being hammered 5-0 by Notts County. He shouted this news to the players from the touchline and somehow Rowley Williams scrambled an equaliser with ten minutes to go. The result meant that Cardiff were now four points behind Birmingham with two games in hand. Crucially they also had a superior goal average.

Another vital factor was that all Cardiff's remaining three games were at home, where the team had been almost invincible that season. On Monday, Blackburn were trounced 3-1 and, despite some nervous moments, Bury were defeated 3-0 the following Saturday. As Birmingham also won their last game of the season, the stage was set for the decider with Leeds. Excitement and anticipation were at fever pitch in the days leading up to the game.

Leeds had enjoyed a good season and, even though John Charles was missing for this match because of an injury, the team was strong enough to finish fifth in the

The two captains, Alf Sherwood (left) and Tommy Burden toss up before the vital promotion match with Leeds. Mr. Pankhurst of Warwick is the referee.

League. Wisely, the City team paid no heed to a light hearted promise made to George Edwards by two Leeds' players: "Don't worry; we're not going to kick you today. We want you to get promotion".

Torrential rain was pouring down on the day of the match and significantly the Bluebirds usually played their best football on heavy pitches. Despite the fact that the Bob-bank was completely open in those days, more than 50,000 people were inside Ninian Park when the game began.

Scott, the Leeds' goalkeeper, dives as a shot from Blair goes just past the post. McCabe and Grant (far right) watch carefully to see where the ball goes.

The headline in the Football Echo celebrates promotion after the match. After 23 years the Bluebirds had returned to Division I.

The City attacked from the start and showed few signs of any nerves. Goalkeeper Scott was a busy man, though Cardiff had a fright when a header from Fidler hit the top of the crossbar before the ball went behind. After 28 minutes came the moment the crowd had been waiting for. **Wilf Grant** beat two players before hitting a left-footed drive which left Scott helpless.

Grant, who had enjoyed such a marvellous season, eased the tension just before half-time when the Leeds defence expected him to pass to Chisholm. Instead he dribbled his way through to score his 26th goal of the season with a shot that went in off the upright. Grant had been signed from Southampton two years earlier as a right winger but had only enjoyed moderate success in that role. His career was transformed in a match against Hull the previous season when, following an injury to a City player, he was moved to centre-forward

In the second half, Cardiff continued to press and after 55 minutes **Ken Chisholm** put the issue beyond doubt with a spectacular header. Rowley Williams crossed the ball from the right and, as Scott came out to intercept it, Chisholm almost leaned backwards to loop the ball over his head. The big Scot had been an inspired signing from Coventry a few weeks earlier when Cardiff's promotion challenge was wobbling and this was his 7th goal in 11 appearances.

With the crowd cheering the team on to Division I football, Cardiff might have scored again but there was only to be one more goal. It came as a consolation for Leeds near the end as **Iggleden** scored off the post. The Bluebirds were back in football's top flight, level with Birmingham on 51 points but with a superior goal difference of 0.14. It was fitting that Cyril Spiers, who had returned to manage the club in 1947 when Billy McCandless moved to Swansea, was at the helm as the Bluebirds completed their post-war revival.

Among the congratulations pouring into the club was a message from the FA of Wales: "Welshmen everywhere rejoice that at last the premier club in Wales is back

A joyful crowd salute the City team after the game with Leeds. Insets show Sir Herbert Merrett and Alf Sherwood addressing the spectators from the Grandstand.

again in its rightful place in League football". At the end of the game jubilant spectators invaded the pitch and Sir Herbert Merrett, the club's president, told them, "We are back where we belong and I can assure you all that we are there to stay". As it turned out, Sir Herbert was too optimistic. The City only spent five years in Division I but, for those who were there, nothing can tarnish the memory of that wet afternoon in May.

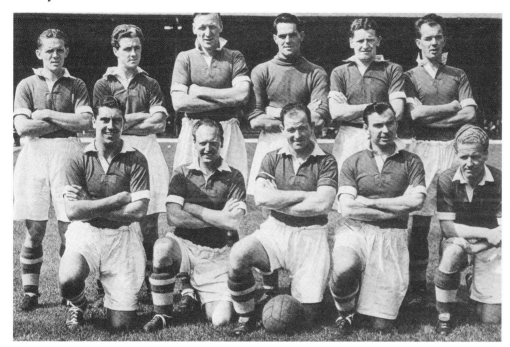

Rowley Williams played in place of Tiddy but otherwise this was the team that defeated Leeds. Back row (left to right); Wilf Grant, Mike Tiddy, Stan Montgomery, Ron Howells, Glyn Williams, Doug Blair. Front row; Ken Chisholm, Billy Baker, Alf Sherwood, George Edwards, Bobby McLaughlin.

Teams:
Cardiff City: Howells; Williams (G), Sherwood; Mcloughlin, Montgomery, Baker; Williams (R), Blair, Grant, Chisholm, Edwards.
Leeds United: Scott; Milburn, Hair; Kerfoot, McCabe, Burden; Harrison, Mills, Fidler, Iggleden, Williams.

An aerial view of Ninian Park during City's game with Arsenal on the night when the crowd record for a club match was broken.

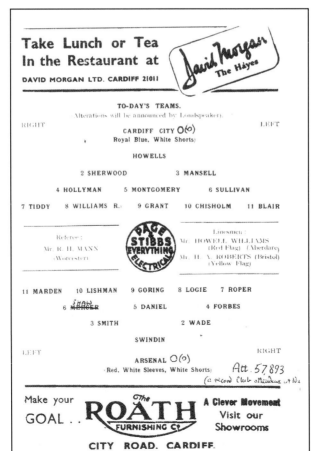

The Cardiff City and Arsenal teams for a match which was keenly contested but ended in a 0-0 draw.

MIXED FORTUNES IN THE 1950S

While the Bluebirds had some great moments in Division I, they all too often struggled and in 1957 poor results at Easter ensured a return to the Second Division. International matches were still great occasions at Ninian Park and in 1958 Wales reached the finals of the World Cup for the first and so far only time. The Welsh Cup Final between the Bluebirds and a fine Swansea team in 1956 drew a record crowd for the competition.

Football League Division I: Wednesday 15 April 1953

Cardiff City (0) 0 Arsenal (0) 0

At the end of February, following a poor run of results, the City appeared to be heading for a rapid return to Division II. The turning point of Cardiff's season came on 7 March when a goal from Doug Blair proved enough to defeat Arsenal at Highbury. It was the start of a good run of results and the Bluebirds could look forward to this return match with the Gunners in the knowledge they were safe from relegation.

Not that this was an end of season game for either side. Arsenal were always an attraction wherever they played but for City supporters there was extra spice with memories of that great day in 1927, and the knowledge that Arsenal had never won at Ninian Park. For the Gunners, involved in a tight race with Preston to win the First Division Championship, the game was vital, while Cardiff had the incentive of completing a notable double over the best team in Division I. So it was no great

Another near miss for Ken Chisholm (left) as he rises to a centre from Grant, only to see the ball cleared off the line.

surprise that a crowd of 57,893, a record for a club match at Ninian Park, packed the ground on a beautiful spring evening for a game of interesting possibilities.

The Arsenal team was filled with gifted players who played entertaining football and ended the season as leading scorers in the First Division. Jimmy Logie, Doug Lishman, Peter Goring and Don Roper all contributed to a tally of 97 goals. Behind them lay a solid defence. Welshman Ray Daniel and Scottish international Alex Forbes were tenacious tacklers, while George Swindin, later a Cardiff manager, was one of the best goalkeepers in the country. At full back for the City was Jack Mansell, a stylish full back signed from Brighton the previous October. He played 24 times for the Bluebirds before moving to Portsmouth. Otherwise the side consisted of players who had been involved in the promotion campaign a year earlier.

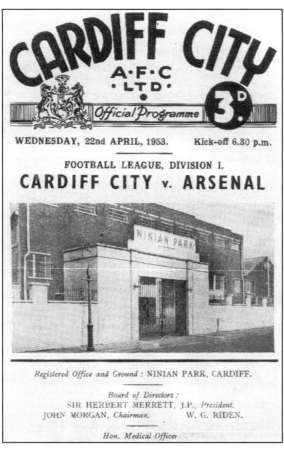

The Gunners began the match in a manner befitting champions-elect but the City defence held firm and, as the first half progressed, the best chances fell to the Bluebirds. After 25 minutes Chisholm beat off the challenge from three defenders and was unlucky enough to see his shot kicked off the line by full-back Wade. Five minutes from half time it was Chisholm again whose goal-bound header was once more scrambled away.

Rowley Williams was having a splendid match and ten minutes after the re-start, he burst through the Arsenal defence. Swindin risked serious injury as he prevented a certain goal with a brave, daring dive to his feet. *Citizen* wrote, "If points were given for near misses City would have been comfortable winners". Yet Arsenal too went close on several occasions and near the end appeared more likely to snatch a winner. Goring missed one good opportunity and five minutes from time Lishman miskicked from six yards with only Howells to beat.

The cover of the programme for the match with Arsenal, showing the entrance to the Grandstand from Sloper Road.

"Fiery Arsenal met their match at Ninian Park" was the *Echo* headline. On a hard ground the game was played at a tremendous pace and a draw was a fair result. Good football was accompanied by exciting goal mouth action and the lack of goals was mainly due to splendid defending by both sides. The Bluebirds were the only team against whom Arsenal failed to score that season and the huge crowd showed its appreciation at the end of the game by giving both teams a standing ovation.

It was a crucial point for Arsenal. Two weeks later they were League Champions for the sixth time, level on points with Preston but with a superior goal average. During the season the City achieved the unusual feat of away wins against both FA Cup finalists, Bolton and Blackpool, and against the League champions and runners up, Arsenal and Preston. It had been a successful season as the team finished a comfortable 12th with the best defensive record in Division I.

Football League Division I: Saturday 30 April 1955

Cardiff City (2) 3 Wolverhampton Wanderers (1) 2

Before this game Cardiff had suffered a disastrous run of results and relegation was a real possibility. With two points from their last ten games, the team had plunged from a safe mid-table position to one in which it was essential to win this final home match. The task could hardly have been more difficult as Wolves, led by England captain Billy Wright, were one of the strongest sides in English football. In glorious sunshine a crowd of 32,000, one of the largest of the season, underlined the importance of this game.

The teams for the match between Wolves and Cardiff. It was a make or break game for the Bluebirds as they fought to remain in Division I.

In a match packed with action, Graham Vearncombe dives at the feet of Denis Wilshaw to save a certain goal.

Making his debut for the City at inside-right was 20 year old Gerry Hitchens. Cardiff had signed him from Kidderminster the previous January and his introduction to the First Division could hardly have been more dramatic. After three minutes Trevor Ford lobbed a perfect ball from the edge of the penalty area to **Hitchens** whose header gave England's international goalkeeper, Bert Williams, no chance.

It was a great start but after 12 minutes the Wolves equalised. Sherwood headed out a cross from Smith into the path of **Denis Wilshaw** who made no mistake with a first time shot. Recent matches suggested that City would crumble after this blow but on this occasion the players showed both their skill and fighting spirit. They regained the lead as Ron Stockin, an ex-Wolves player, passed to **Trevor Ford** who fired the ball into the net from 15 yards. Three goals had been scored in 18 minutes and both sides had enough chances to add a few more before half-time.

Billy Wright was having difficulty in containing Ford and the Bluebirds continued to bombard the Wolves' goal in the second half. Their enemy was anxiety as Wolves fought their way back into the game. There was a heart stopping moment when Vearncombe misjudged a cross from Hancocks and pushed the ball against the underside of the cross bar. Fortunately Sherwood was at hand to clear the danger. Jangling nerves were soothed 15 minutes from the end when **Ford** collected a pass from Alan Harrington and beat Williams from close range. Wolves never gave up and two minutes from the end **Flowers** scored with a shot from 20 yards that cannoned off two City players. Then came the news that Leicester were losing 3-1 at Huddersfield and would be relegated with Sheffield Wednesday. At the end of a pulsating match, the cheers of the crowd expressed both relief and jubilation.

Trevor Ford is hidden behind Billy Wright who can only watch as Bert Williams makes a despairing leap in an attempt to prevent City's third goal.

It was a great day for Gerry Hitchens who proved to be a brilliant signing. Over the next two years he was City's leading goal scorer with 41 goals in 99 matches but in December 1957 he was transferred to Aston Villa for £22,500. He was an equally prolific scorer for the Villa, netting five goals in one match against Charlton. Hitchens won seven international caps for England and in 1961 he enjoyed further success in Italy with Inter Milan and Torino. Sadly in 1983 Gerry died from a heart attack at the young age of 48 while he was playing in a charity match.

The other hero of the afternoon was Trevor Ford who led the forward line magnificently. Signed in November 1953 for a club record fee of £30,000, Ford scored more than 50 goals for the Bluebirds, many of them spectacular and some of them vital as in this match. A fiery character, his career at Cardiff did not always run smoothly and in 1957 he left the club after quarrelling with the manager, Trevor

Morris. Soon afterwards allegations he made in his autobiography, *I lead the attack*, led to his suspension by the Football League.

City played Wolves twice more in 1955. In September they returned to Ninian Park and gained revenge by inflicting a record home defeat on the Bluebirds. A rampant Wanderers team won the match 9-1 and it seemed the triumph of the previous April had only delayed relegation for one more season. Yet, when the sides met at Wolverhampton for the return game in December, Cardiff ignored the form book, won the match 2-0, and began a run of results that took them to safety. Such are the twists and turns that make football the game it is.

Gerry Hitchens had an outstanding debut for Cardiff against Wolves. Alf Sherwood said, "His goal was the inspiration we needed". The photograph shows him playing in his last game for the City against Fulham.

Welsh Cup Final: Monday 30 April 1956

Cardiff City (2) 3 Swansea Town (0) 2

Normally the Football League teams in Wales did not take the Welsh Cup seriously, even though the Welsh FA insisted on them playing their strongest teams. Welsh cup-ties, even the final, were rarely crowd pullers yet a record attendance of 37,500 attended this match. On this occasion, the League season was over and the traditional rivalry between Cardiff and Swansea would ensure a keenly fought contest especially as the two sides had not met for four years.

As the First Division team, the Bluebirds were the favourites. In addition the Welsh FA had given them ground advantage on the basis that Ninian Park was the only stadium big enough for a match of this importance. Yet the Swans were far from underdogs. They had enjoyed a good season in Division II and their free scoring forward line had netted 83 goals.

The two captains, Ivor Allchurch and Trevor Ford, toss up before the Welsh Cup Final begins. Referee B.M. Griffiths was officiating at his last match.

It was a time when Swansea produced a conveyor belt of great players, none of whom was greater than Ivor Allchurch, one of the finest inside forwards of his generation. The Bluebirds cast envious eyes on him for years and, when he finally signed for them, he put in many fine performances even though his best years were behind him. Other distinguished players in the Swansea team were Cliff Jones, Mel Charles and Len Allchurch, Ivor's brother. One name missing was that of Terry Medwin who was about to sign for Spurs.

There was a rare moment before the kick-off when the referee, B.M. Griffiths, was given a great reception by the crowd. It was a recognition of the prestige Mr. Griffiths had brought to Wales. This was his last game in a distinguished career in which he had refereed in the World Cup and the FA Cup Final.

The Bluebirds soon took control of the game and after 15 minutes Ford brilliantly beat Charles and Kiley before giving a perfect pass to **Walsh**, whose fierce drive left King helpless. After half an hour the Bluebirds were reduced to ten men as Harry Kirtley broke his leg. In shooting for goal, he accidentally collided with a Swansea player and fractured his tibia. Kirtley was a stylish inside forward who had been a mainstay of the City attack throughout the season and, without the option of a substitute, Cardiff might have crumbled. As it was the team redoubled its efforts and **John McSeveney** scored a second goal just before half-time.

John McSeveney heads a cross from Brian Walsh past Johnny King in the Swansea goal to give the Bluebirds a 2-0 lead.

Two minutes after the interval the game appeared to be over when **Walsh** made the score 3-0 after Stitfall had made a powerful run down the right wing. As the game went on, Cardiff's ten men began to tire but stubborn defending by Harrington, Stitfall and Sullivan kept Swansea at bay until 12 minutes from time, when **Kiley** reduced the arrears with a powerful header from a corner. There was still time for more drama in this exciting climax to the season. First there was a pitch invasion when the crowd mistakenly thought Mr. Griffiths had blown for time. The field was eventually cleared and in the final seconds of the game **Palmer** met a cross from Cliff Jones to snatch another consolation goal for Swansea.

As Trevor Ford triumphantly held up the Welsh Cup, hopes were high that the City were at last established in the First Division. However, the 1956-57 season was to be a bitter disappointment ending in relegation. Ford left the club under a cloud and

Trevor Ford was a great believer in the old-fashioned shoulder charge. Here he is about to launch himself at Johnny King who already has the ball. Gerry Hitchens (right) looks on with interest.

City players celebrate after winning the Welsh Cup. Back row (from left to right); Harrington, Vearncombe, Hitchens. Front row; Stitfall, Sullivan, Malloy, McSeveney, Baker, Walsh and Ford.

Kirtley never recovered from his injury against Swansea. They were both missed but so was the steadying influence of Alf Sherwood. At the age of 33, he no longer commanded a regular place in the team. Believing his career was far from finished, he demanded a transfer and signed for Newport, where he played 205 games and collected two more Welsh caps. It appears that Alf was right and Newport's gain was Cardiff's loss.

Teams:
Cardiff City: Vearncombe; Stitfall, Sullivan; Harrington, Malloy, Baker; Walsh, Kirtley, Ford, Hitchens, McSeveney.
Swansea Town: King; Willis, Thomas; Charles, Kiley, Jones (B); Allchurch (L), Griffiths, Palmer, Allchuch (I), Jones (C).

Football League Division II: 28 December 1957

Cardiff City (5) 6 Liverpool (0) 1

The Bluebirds made a dreadful start to their first season back in Division II. They won only two of their first 11 matches and were languishing near the relegation zone in early December. The team then showed its potential with a remarkable run of victories at Ninian Park, in which 18 goals were scored in three successive home matches.

The cover of the programme for the match between Cardiff and Liverpool. Protection from the elements was still limited but, when the "Bob Bank" was covered the following year, the ground offered shelter on all four sides.

Barnsley were slaughtered 7-0, Stoke were hammered 5-2 on Boxing Day and, for this last match of 1957, a crowd of 30,000 turned up to see how City would fare against the League leaders, Liverpool.

From the outset, Cardiff launched an all-out assault. After only five minutes clever inter-passing between Brayley Reynolds and Ron Hewitt gave **Colin Hudson** an opening and from 15 yards he made no mistake. Earlier in the day he was married so perhaps it was appropriate that he should celebrate his wedding with the best goal of the match.

Few among the crowd expected the goal feast that now followed. After 18 minutes a pass from Brian Walsh gave **Ron Hewitt** the chance

to give City a 2-0 advantage. Before half-time three more goals followed, all of them assisted by a series of defensive blunders, particularly from Tommy Younger, a Scottish international goalkeeper. After half an hour he allowed a weak effort from **Reynolds** to slip off his shoulder and over his head into the net. Two minutes later Younger missed a back pass and **Joe Bonson** nipped in to make it 4-0. Just before the interval **Reynolds** intercepted another poor back pass to the goalkeeper, this time from White, so that Cardiff led 5-0.

On this occasion Hudson is crowded out by two Liverpool defenders. As his shot flies wide of the goal, Younger looks relieved.

The second half proved to be an anti-climax. Liverpool showed what a good side they could be and Liddell was unlucky when his shot hit the post. Yet again the unfortunate Younger was at fault after 77 minutes, when he failed to parry a shot from **Bonson** who scored from the rebound. Seconds from the end, **Wheeler** scored the consolation goal Liverpool deserved when his shot deceived Jones and dipped under the bar.

It was an excellent result though the Bluebirds were flattered by the score-line which probably haunted Younger for weeks afterwards. The game proved to be a springboard for a good cup run in which the City reached the fifth round before going out to Blackburn. Despite their purple patch in December, the team continued to be far too inconsistent in the League and ended the season in 15th place.

The encounter marked the beginning of an extraordinary sequence which established Cardiff as Liverpool's bogy team for the next couple of years. The match was the first of five successive victories, the last of which was a 4-0 City success at

Anfield in December 1959. After that the teams avoided each other until October 2007 when they met in the Carling Cup. Any hopes that the bogy might still work were dispelled as Liverpool triumphed 2-1.

Ron Hewitt replaced Nugent, but otherwise this was the team that crushed Liverpool 6-1. Back row (left to right); Brian Walsh, Alan Harrington, Ken Jones, Danny Malloy, Alec Milne, Colin Baker. Front row; Joe Bonson, Brayley Reynolds, Ron Stitfall, Colin Hudson, Cliff Nugent.

Teams:
Cardiff City: Jones; Stitfall, Milne; Harrington, Malloy, Baker; Walsh, Hewitt, Bonson, Reynolds, Hudson.
Liverpool: Younger; Molyneux, Moran; Wheeler, White, Campbell (D); McNamara, Rowley, Liddell, Murdoch, A'Court.

World Cup Qualifier: Wednesday 5 February 1958

Wales (0) 2 Israel (0) 0

Fortune smiled on Wales when the nation made what has so far been its only appearance in the finals of the World Cup. The team failed to win its group but were given a second chance when Arab countries, for political reasons, refused to play Israel. FIFA ruled that Israel would have to play one of the seven runners-up from the European groups and, in the lottery that followed, Wales were the lucky beneficiaries.

In January 1958 the team travelled to Tel Aviv for the first leg of the match and the troubled atmosphere of Israel was indicated by the tank tracks marking the pitch. In a sweltering temperature of 80 degrees, Wales were comfortable 2-0 winners to record their first away victory against a foreign country.

The return game at Ninian Park, played in cold, wet conditions, was never a classic. Wales dominated play from the start and the Israeli goalkeeper and captain, Yacov

Chodoroff, made four great saves in the first 20 minutes. Outclassed, the Israelis decided to stop the Welsh team by resorting to blatant obstruction and scything tackles. For much of the game they succeeded and John Charles came in for some particularly harsh treatment which could have resulted in serious injury. The Dutch referee, Klas Schipper, showed far too much leniency and took no action beyond awarding Wales a succession of free kicks.

When the Welsh forwards had a sight of goal, it was the brilliant Chodoroff who kept them at bay. Ironically, with 20 minutes to go and a dreary

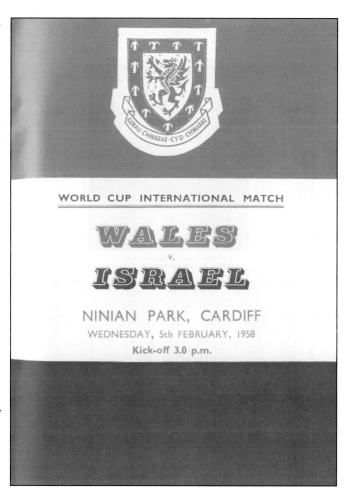

The programme for the vital World Cup Qualifying match between Wales and Israel. Victory took the Welsh team to the finals.

goal-less draw looking inevitable, he suffered the worst injury of the afternoon. He and John Charles both jumped for a high ball and the goalkeeper came off worst. Despite suffering from concussion, a broken nose and a sprained shoulder, he remained in goal. He was still dazed when **Ivor Allchurch** beat four Israeli defenders in the penalty area to score a brilliant goal from a seemingly impossible angle. It was academic when **Cliff Jones** netted the second after Hewitt and Medwin had split the defence.

Despite the crude tactics of his team, Chodoroff was the hero of the match and was given a standing ovation from the crowd as he left the field. He knew nothing about it and could not even remember the score or where he was. Little more than semi-conscious, he was taken to St. David's Hospital where he spoke to the nurses in Hebrew, convinced he was back in Israel.

Wales were in the World Cup finals and much of the credit for that success was due to Jimmy Murphy, the assistant manager of Manchester United. He and Matt Busby had built up the legendary team that became the "Busby Babes" and in 1957 Murphy was invited to become the Welsh coach. At once he brought that "Manchester United-like spirit" to the Welsh squad.

When Murphy returned to Manchester the day after the match with Israel, he was greeted with the tragic news of the Munich air crash in which eight players died and

John Charles looks on in amazement as Israel's goalkeeper, Chodoroff, makes another fine save to keep his side in the game.

Matt Busby was seriously injured. Despite his grief, it was Jimmy who began to rebuild Manchester United and amazingly his patched up team reached the Cup Final, only to lose 2-0 at the last hurdle against Bolton Wanderers.

In June Wales went to Sweden very much the underdogs but Jimmy Murphy's inspiration and passion inspired his team to astonish the football world with their performances. After drawing all three of their group matches, Wales beat Hungary 2-1

Jimmy Murphy emphasises a point to his Welsh players. As Cliff Jones said: "He had this wonderful gift of making everyone feel relaxed and part of a unique set-up".

in a play-off to reach the quarter finals. Unfortunately, the brutal treatment meted out to John Charles by the Hungarians ended his part in the competition. In the quarter-finals Wales played the eventual winners, Brazil, without their star player and lost the game by a solitary goal. Though their quest for glory had ended in defeat, the 1958 World Cup still represents the greatest triumph in the history of Welsh football.

Teams:

Wales: Kelsey; Williams, Hopkins; Harrington, Charles (M), Bowen; Medwin, Hewitt, Charles (J), Allchurch, Jones.

Israel: Chodoroff; Lefkovitz, Morcechovitz; Amar, Reznik, Tisch; Nahmias, Stelnach, Gegossian, Goldstein, Glazer.

The team that defeated Israel. Back row (left to right); Alan Harrington, Stuart Williams, John Charles, Jack Kelsey, Mel Hopkins, Ivor Allchurch, Mel Charles. Front row; Terry Medwin, Ron Hewitt, Dave Bowen, Cliff Jones.

J.C. Walker provides a topical cartoon for City's promotion clash at the Easter weekend with Aston Villa.

Graham Moore enjoyed a meteoric rise to stardom in City's promotion campaign of 1960. Moreover, he was selected to play for Wales against England after only a handful of League games and scored the equalising Welsh goal.

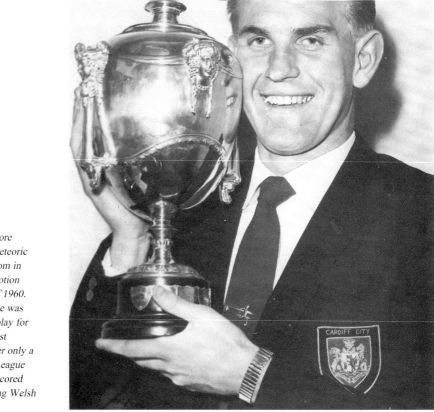

ANOTHER BRIEF SPELL IN DIVISION I

After spending three years in the Second Division, Cardiff once more gained promotion in 1960. The team enjoyed some notable successes in their first season back in Division I but the following year a disastrous run after Christmas once more doomed them to relegation.

Football League Division II: 16 April 1960

Cardiff City (1) 1 Aston Villa (0) 0

This match was a celebration of Cardiff City's Golden Jubilee and victory would take the Bluebirds back to the First Division. Aston Villa had already won promotion and much of the interest in the game centred on whether Villa or Cardiff would be the Second Division Champions.

Despite a couple of heavy defeats recently, Cardiff had played entertaining football throughout the season. Manager Bill Jones and his coach, Wilf Grant, a hero of Cardiff's last promotion campaign, devised a method of attacking football that served the side well. The inside forwards were the spearhead of the attack, while the wingers and the centre-forward played more deeply behind them. The fact that Cardiff finished the season with 90 goals is proof of how successful the plan was.

Derek Tapscott, signed by Bill Jones from Arsenal, scored 20 goals and Joe Bonson, the other inside forward, added another 18. Wingers John Watkins, another of Jones's astute signings, and Brian Walsh gave them excellent support, but the star of the season was 19 year old Graham Moore. In his first full season, Moore not only scored 16 goals but, as a deep-lying, roaming centre-forward, he provided numerous opportunities for his colleagues.

Earlier in the season City had lost a thrilling encounter 2-0 at Villa Park. On a beautiful sunny afternoon a crowd of 55,000 packed into Ninian Park to see if Cardiff could avenge that defeat and clinch promotion. Gerry Hitchens, the former City player, who had contributed so much to Villa's promotion charge, was injured and

The only goal of the game with Aston Villa was scored by Graham Moore, whose full-blooded drive left goalkeeper Sims helpless.

Nigel Sims clutches the ball to his chest as Derek Tapscott, hoping for a rebound, races in to challenge.

missed the game. The Bluebirds were also forced to make a change as Bonson was unfit and his place was taken by Colin Hudson.

The game was played in an electrifying atmosphere which seemed to affect both teams. Neither of them produced the free flowing football that had characterised their play throughout the season. Passes often went astray and defences were generally on top. However there was plenty of incident to keep the crowd on its toes and Hudson was guilty of missing a golden opportunity to put the City ahead after seven minutes.

When the winning goal came after 13 minutes it was worthy of the occasion. Brian Walsh, receiving the ball from Nicholls, slipped a pass to Hudson who centred for **Moore** to unleash a tremendous shot from 12 yards.

The City continued to create chances but the visitors too had their opportunities. When they won a free kick just outside the Cardiff penalty area, Peter McParland's attempt to outwit Cardiff's defensive wall was blocked by Ron Stitfall. Moments before half-time McParland had an even better chance when he faced an open goal, only to land his shot on top of the Canton Stand.

In the second half, Villa pressed hard for an equalising goal but the Cardiff defence, well marshalled by Danny Malloy, held firm. The Bluebirds' attacks were less frequent, but they were twice denied reasonable appeals for a penalty as the game became more robust. All the Cardiff players fell back to their own penalty area as Villa launched a furious onslaught on the City goal in the closing minutes. Supporters began frantically whistling as the 90 minutes were up but the referee, Mr. Rogers, insisted on adding two more for stoppages.

As the game ended a mighty roar went up and the crowd flooded on to the field, repeating the scenes of eight years earlier when the Bluebirds defeated Leeds. Despite their defeat, the Villa fans and their supporters could afford to be generous. They too were guaranteed promotion and Joe Mercer, the Villa manager, praised the City team for the "great football they had played throughout the season".

Cardiff's chairman, Ron Beecher, paid tribute to his manager: "What an asset we have at Ninian Park in the man who has inculcated a team spirit second to none in the land". Bill Jones was a quiet, unassuming man who did not believe in making rash predictions. He had banned any talk of promotion in the dressing room and was now

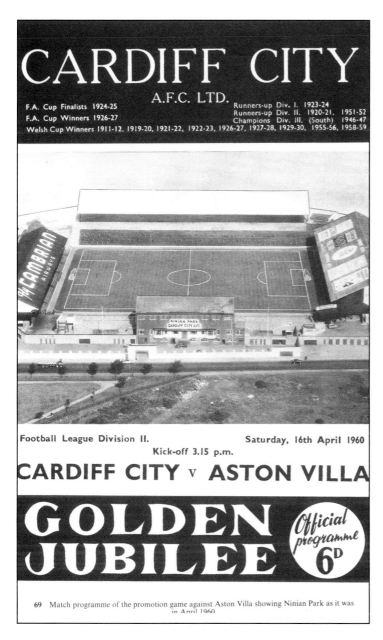

CARDIFF CITY

A.F.C. LTD.

F.A. Cup Finalists 1924-25   Runners-up Div. I. 1923-24
F.A. Cup Winners 1926-27   Runners-up Div. II. 1920-21, 1951-52
Welsh Cup Winners 1911-12, 1919-20, 1921-22, 1922-23, 1926-27, 1927-28, 1929-30, 1955-56, 1958-59   Champions Div. III. (South) 1946-47

Football League Division II.   Saturday, 16th April 1960
Kick-off 3.15 p.m.

CARDIFF CITY v ASTON VILLA

GOLDEN JUBILEE

Official programme 6ᴅ

69   Match programme of the promotion game against Aston Villa showing Ninian Park as it was in April 1960

The programme for this Jubilee game may have brought back memories to the older members in the crowd of that day in 1910, when Villa were the visitors in the first game to be played at Ninian Park.

wise enough to warn: "Next year it will be twice as hard staying up as it has been getting there".

Wilf Grant said: "It's been a wonderful climax to a wonderful season – now let's hope we can snatch that championship". The result left the City one point ahead of Villa but the team threw away the chance to be champions two days later when, in a very disappointing performance, they lost 1-0 at home to Plymouth.

Teams:
Cardiff City: Nicholls; Milne, Stitfall; Gammon, Malloy, Baker; Walsh, Tapscott, Moore, Hudson, Watkins.
Aston Villa; Sims; Lynn, Neal; Crowe, Dugdale, Saward; Adam, Thomson, Dixon, Wylie, McParland.

Football League Division I:
Saturday 26 November 1960

Cardiff City (2) 3 Manchester United (0) 0

Manchester United were visiting Ninian Park for the first time since the Munich air crash had shattered the magnificent "Busby Babes". Before the match both clubs, with 13 points from 18 games, were too close to the relegation zone for comfort. The floodlights, installed at the beginning of the season, proved their value on a dark, wintry afternoon. The entire game was played in a torrential downpour and the appalling weather kept the crowd down to a disappointing 21,000. Mr. Horner, the referee, only decided the match could go ahead 45 minutes before the kick-off.

> **LEST WE FORGET**
>
> **A Tribute from The Cardiff City Football Club and their followers.**
>
> November is the month when we remember the dead of two world wars. It is appropriate therefore, to think back for a moment and remember also those officials and players of the Manchester United Football Club together with pressmen and others who died in the air disaster at Munich on February 6th, 1958.
>
> There was Walter Crickman, who, at the time of his death, was one of the best known and most popular club secretaries in the land. He served United for 38 years and was the recipient of the Football League's Gold Medal for outstanding service. Tom Curry and Bert Whalley, Trainer and Assistant Trainer who between them served the Club for 44 years. Two fine men of outstanding character.
>
> And when we turn to those wonderful players, even for those who had no connection with United, it was a tragedy felt and shared by all.
>
> Roger Byrne, Duncan Edwards, Tommy Taylor, David Pegg, Eddie Colman, Bill Whelan, Mark Jones, Geoffrey Bent. Of these, all were killed except Duncan Edwards who died on 21st February. 1958.
>
> Sportswriters, eight of them, died with the boys they went to write about and one of them, Henry Rose, was a Cardiff product. Alf Clarke (*Evening Chronicle*), Tom Jackson (*Evening News*), Eric Thompson (*Daily Mail*), Henry Rose (*Daily Express*), Don Davies (*Manchester Guardian*), Arch Ledbrooke (*Daily Mirror*), George Follows (*Daily Herald*) and Frank Swift (*News of the World*).
>
> This terrible disaster which happened a little less than three years ago took a terrible toll and today, when we play Manchester United for the first time since that happening we remember with reverence and respect.
>
> On a happier note we also pay tribute to the resilience of the Club and its famous manager and we are happy that those who survived are still playing a full part in the affairs of Manchester United.

When Manchester United came to Ninian Park in November 1960, Matt Busby was still rebuilding his team from the ashes of Munich. The programme notes paid a moving tribute both to him and his famous club.

The Bluebirds soon brought the crowd to life with their best display of the season. Scintillating attacks ripped the United defence apart and only a series of wonderful saves from Harry Gregg kept the score-sheet blank in the opening stages. Yet Manchester almost took the lead with a bizarre goal when Violet injured his shoulder after clashing with a City defender. As he lay on the ground, a shot from Charlton flew across the goal, struck Violet and bounced towards the goal, sticking in the mud just short of the line. Soon afterwards Violet was forced to retire with a fractured collar bone. His absence severely handicapped United but even before this accident the Bluebirds were well on top.

Wingers Brian Walsh and Derek Hogg, both of them in dazzling form, were the stars of the City attack. In this match Walsh was marked by Noel Cantwell, who had just signed for United. Cantwell had always found it difficult to play against Walsh and, as the Cardiff winger tormented him, there must have been moments when the Irish international regretted he had not delayed his transfer a few days longer.

Derek Hogg was a tricky winger who loved to take on the opposing full back. Sometimes accused of being over elaborate,

The team sheet for the match with Manchester United. Harry Gregg, Bill Foulkes, Denis Violet and Bobby Charlton were the only survivors from the Munich tragedy playing in this game

it was he who put the City ahead after half an hour. A corner from Walsh found Brian Edgley whose perfect cross was met by **Hogg**. United, inspired by Bobby Charlton, rallied for a time but it was the Bluebirds who scored again just before half-time. Watkins supplied a perfect centre to **Edgley** whose powerful drive left Gregg helpless. It was the only goal Edgley ever scored for Cardiff. Recently signed from Shrewsbury he made only a handful of appearances before moving on to Brentford at the end of the season.

Cardiff dominated the second half but United's ten men ensured there would be no rout. A controversial third goal came when Tapscott chased a long clearance from Malloy. With United defenders appealing for offside, he collided with Gregg in mid-air and, as the ball ran loose, **Hogg** calmly netted his second goal of the afternoon. Tempers began to fray in the closing minutes and, as crunching tackles flew in, Dawson was warned after a bad foul on Malloy. United never gave up and Charlton was unlucky when his shot beat Vearncombe, only to hit the bar.

Brian Walsh joined Cardiff from Arsenal in 1955 and for six years entertained the crowd with his brilliant ball control and his ability to beat an opponent. Against United he produced one of his greatest performances for the club.

Alex Dawson (number 9) fails to reach the target with a flying header as United looked for a consolation goal late in the game.

What one reporter described as "a glorious mudlark" showed how footballers of that era could entertain even in the most atrocious conditions. Matt Busby was generous in praising the Cardiff performance as the team began to steadily climb the League table. Manchester United eventually finished in 7th place as Busby continued the process of creating another great side that would once more see United as one of the leading clubs in the land.

Football League Division I: Saturday 11 March 1961

Cardiff City (1) 3 Tottenham Hotspur (2) 2

This was one of the greatest Saturdays in Cardiff's sporting history. On a beautiful spring day, 100,000 rugby and football fans flooded into the city. In the afternoon the international match between Wales and Ireland at the Cardiff Arms Park proved to be something of an anti-climax, despite a Welsh victory by nine points to nil.

The game against Tottenham Hotspur in the evening was a very different story. A crowd of 45,580 came to see the Bluebirds test themselves against the Spurs, who were hot favourites to become the first team in the 20th century to achieve the double of the First Division Championship and the FA Cup. Before the match Tottenham, with 53 points from 31 games, had already virtually clinched the Championship.

Moreover Spurs were the great entertainers. Their captain, Danny Blanchflower, was a mercurial Irishman who had definite views about football. "The great fallacy is first and last about winning … football is about glory … doing things in style with a

The teams for that great match between Cardiff and Tottenham. The Spurs' side was filled with talented players who at times that season appeared almost invincible.

flourish … beating the other lot without waiting for them to die of boredom". That Spurs' team was never boring. It was filled with inventive international stars, among them John White and Dave MacKay, the iron man of the team. Cliff Jones from Swansea was the finest winger in the country, while Bobby Smith was an old fashioned centre forward and the team's leading scorer. At the end of the season this array of talent had scored an amazing 136 goals in League and Cup matches.

Earlier in the season Cardiff had lost an entertaining match at White Hart Lane 3-2. Since that time the team had moved into the top half of the table with a number of

Dave Mackay and Graham Moore have an argument in the game with Spurs. Alan Harrington tries to separate them, while Ron Stitfall and Danny Malloy appear uncertain whether to join in or act as peacemakers.

Derek Tapscott (left) pushes the ball into the Tottenham net for what proved to be the winning goal.

City goalkeeper Ron Nicholls, supported by Malloy, punches the ball clear from a Tottenham attack. Bobby Smith (left) and Mackay are the Spurs players waiting for a mistake.

impressive displays but few expected them to overcome a Tottenham side that had only tasted defeat three times that season.

People were still filing into the ground when Spurs took the lead in their first attack as **Terry Dyson** collected a pass from White to sweep the ball just inside the post. In the 11th minute Cardiff equalised with a brilliant goal through **Derek Hogg**. He collected the ball in his own half and beat three Spurs' players before launching a tremendous shot into the roof of the net. Tottenham soon regained the lead as goalkeeper Nicholls could only palm away a cross from Smith into the path of **Les Allen**. At half-time Spurs deservedly led 2-1 and had displayed all the poise and fluent skills which had been the hallmark of their season.

Within five minutes of the restart, the game was transformed. First, **Walsh** once more brought the score-line level as he cut in from the right wing to beat goalkeeper Brown with a fine shot. That was exciting enough, but two minutes later the cheering reached a new crescendo as an unmarked **Tapscott** was fed a perfect pass from Barry Hole and slid the ball home for what proved to be the winner. In the remaining 35 minutes or so, the City defence lived dangerously at times. Nicholls dropped the ball more than once but a defender was always on hand to boot it clear. As the game ended the crowd rose to its feet and gave a standing ovation to both sides after what had been for me the best game I ever saw.

Danny Malloy, signed from Dundee United in 1955, played 242 games for Cardiff City. His display against Spurs was among his best.

It was one of those contests when the man of the match could have been anyone on the field but, in the latter stages of the game, Danny Malloy at centre-half marshalled the defence superbly, as Spurs threw everything into the search for a late equaliser. Graham Moore, with his outstanding ball distribution skills, was also outstanding and an inspiration to the other City forwards.

The writer of the City match programme showed shrewd foresight when he commented: "I reckon to see the best game of football yet so far this season at Ninian Park and we could very well provide a great shock". Ever the great sportsman, Danny Blanchflower paid tribute to, "A fine Cardiff showing … the most improved side in the First Division". Peter Corrigan wrote in the *South Wales Echo*: "I've never known such excitement, such nerve-racking moments, such voluble elation at what was after all only a League game". Even rugby fans, who had made their way to Ninian Park after the match in the afternoon, were impressed. One said, "What I saw tonight, compared with this afternoon, means Ninian Park has got another spectator".

Spurs soon shook off this setback and went on to win the League, eight points ahead of Sheffield Wednesday. Truly a magnificent team as they completed the double by defeating Leicester 2-0 at Wembley. The win took the Bluebirds up to 6th place in Division I but sadly their form deteriorated as they failed to win another match that season. Yet the memory of that momentous victory against Tottenham is something those who were there will never forget.

Football League Division I: Monday 23 April 1962

Cardiff City (2) 3 West Ham United (0) 0

At the start of the season hopes were high that the Bluebirds would consolidate their position in Division I. On 7 November, following a 2-1 victory over Sheffield

OFFICIAL 4ᴰ· PROGRAMME

CARDIFF CITY

A.F.C. LTD.

Runners-up Div. I. 1923-24
Runners-up Div. II. 1920-21, 1951-52, 1959-60
Champions Div. III. (South) 1946-47
Welsh Cup Winners 1911-12, 1919-20, 1921-22, 1922-23, 1926-27, 1927-28, 1929-30, 1955-56, 1958-59

F.A. Cup Finalists 1924-25
F.A. Cup Winners 1926-27

Captain Morgan Rum
the right rum for today's taste

Football League Division I.   Monday, 23rd April 1962.

Kick-off 3.15 p.m.

CARDIFF CITY   v   WEST HAM UNITED

Board of Directors - R. BEECHER (Chairman)   F. T. DEWEY, J.P.,   G. EDWARDS, M.A.
Manager: W. JONES   Secretary: G. KEENOR

The programme for City's last game in the First Division. The picture of Ninian Park shows the stand covering the popular bank with its Captain Morgan advertisement. The floodlights were installed two years earlier.

Wednesday, the team occupied seventh place in the table. What followed was a disastrous run of 21 matches, only one of which was won, until a 3-2 victory over Birmingham on 21 April broke the depressing sequence. Two days later on Easter Monday, West Ham were the visitors for City's last home game of the season.

On Good Friday the Hammers had easily beaten Cardiff 4-1 at Upton Park. In their team for this return match were Bobby Moore, Martin Peters, and Geoff Hurst, all of whom would figure in England's World Cup winning side of 1966. There were several faces missing in the Cardiff side compared with a year earlier. In particular the team missed the clever distribution skills of Graham Moore who was transferred to Chelsea, and the stout-hearted defending of Danny Malloy who became player-coach at Doncaster.

Though relegation appeared inevitable, Cardiff proved to be too good for West Ham in their last home match. This superb header from Dai Ward gave them an early lead.

Their replacements had ability but failed to make an impact in time to halt Cardiff's decline.

Needing a miracle to escape relegation, a crowd of about 10,000 was depressing evidence that the fans had written off City's chances of First Division survival. Yet those who stayed away missed one of the team's best displays of the season. After only five minutes **Dai Ward** gave the Bluebirds the lead when a speculative cross from Tapscott found him unmarked. Cardiff continued to dominate the game, and it was no surprise when Tapscott was once more the provider for **Ward** to score again from close range in the 37th minute.

The Hammers rarely looked like scoring and played as though the end of the season could not come quickly enough. They suffered a further blow when their goal keeper, Brian Rhodes, was carried off with a dislocated collar bone. With West Ham down to ten men, Martin Peters replaced him in goal but 20 minutes from the end he could do nothing to keep out **Tapscott's** diving header.

Tapscott (number 8) sees his header blocked by West Ham's Bobby Moore as the Bluebirds belatedly found their form.

Tapscott and Ward, who had been out of favour recently, made the most of their recall to the team. Tapscott had scored a hat trick against Birmingham and in this match continued his welcome return to form. Ward, signed from Bristol Rovers a year earlier, was only playing because Mel Charles was injured. He led the forward line well and ended the season as Cardiff's leading scorer with 17 goals. Ron Stitfall, making only his third appearance of the season, was the pick of the defenders. Though he had reached the veteran stage, the team might have benefited if he had been selected more often. One of the finest full-backs to play for the Bluebirds, Stitfall's career with the City spanned 18 years until his retirement in 1965.

After their displays against Birmingham and West Ham, it was hard to understand why the City players had not shown this kind of spirit earlier. As news filtered through that Fulham, City's nearest rivals, had lost 3-0 at West Bromwich, it seemed that this last desperate effort might yet preserve Cardiff's Division I status. Any lingering hopes of that sort vanished the following Saturday when the Bluebirds were thrashed 8-3 by Everton.

Manager Bill Jones commented after the game with West Ham: "The ball ran for us, but when we really needed the breaks earlier in the season, we could not get them". This was only partially true. A few weeks earlier, in a vital encounter with Fulham, Cardiff gave a pathetic display in losing 3-0. City's players may have reflected on that result as the Bluebirds ended the season just one point behind the Londoners. Their brief stay in Division I was over and they have not returned since.

Cardiff's results tell the miserable story of the 1961-62 season. A dying flourish at Easter could not hide the inept displays of the previous months.

PAGE TWELVE

FOOTBALL LEAGUE, DIVISION 1

1961 — Goals

Aug.			F	A
19	Blackburn Rovers	A	0	0
23	Sheffield United	H	1	1
26	Blackpool	H	3	2
28	Sheffield United	A	0	1
Sept.				
2	Tottenham Hotspur	A	2	3
6	Chelsea	H	5	2
9	Bolton Wanderers	H	1	2
16	Manchester United	H	1	2
20	Chelsea	A	3	2
23	Wolverhampton Wanderers	A	1	1
30	Nottingham Forest	H	2	2
Oct.				
7	Manchester City	A	2	1
14	Wales v. England	H	1	1
18	West Bromwich Albion	H	2	2
21	Burnley	A	1	2
28	Arsenal	H	1	1
Nov.				
4	(1) Fulham	A	1	0
11	Sheffield Wednesday	H	2	1
18	Leicester City	A	0	3
25	(2) Ipswich Town	H	0	3
Dec.				
2	Birmingham City	A	0	3
9	Everton	H	0	0
16	Blackburn Rovers	H	1	1
23	Blackpool	A	0	3
26	Aston Villa	H	1	0

1962

Jan.				
10	(3) Middlesbrough (Cup)	A	0	1
13	Tottenham Hotspur	H	1	1
20	Bolton Wanderers	A	1	1
27	(4)			
Feb.				
3	Manchester United	A	0	3
9	Wolverhampton Wanderers	H	2	3
17	(5) Nottingham Forest	A	1	2
24	Manchester City	H	0	0
March				
3	West Bromwich Albion	A	1	5
14	Burnley	H	1	1
17	Arsenal	A	1	1
23	Fulham	H	0	3
April				
3	Sheffield Wednesday	A	0	2
7	Leicester City	H	0	4
14	Ipswich Town	A	0	1
20	West Ham United	A		
21	Birmingham City	H		
23	West Ham United	H		
28	Everton	A		
May				
5	Cup Final			

FOOTBALL COMBINATION

1961 — Goals

Aug.			F	A
19	Norwich City	H	3	0
26	West Ham United	A	2	5
Sept.				
2	Tottenham Hotspur	H	1	3
9	Shrewsbury Town	A	6	0
16	Crystal Palace	A	2	2
23	Northampton Town	H	4	0
30	Nottingham Forest	A	1	2
Oct.				
7	Arsenal	H	5	6
14	Plymouth Argyle	A	0	4
21	Ipswich Town	H	2	0
28	Leicester City	A	1	3
Nov.				
4	Luton Town	H	0	0
11	Notts County	A	1	3
18	Mansfield Town	H	3	0
25	Peterborough United	A	3	1
Dec.				
2	Plymouth Argyle	H	4	0
9	Arsenal	A	1	5
16	Norwich City	A	0	1
23	West Ham United	H	3	4

1962

Jan.				
13	Tottenham Hotspur	A	1	4
20	Shrewsbury Town	H	2	2
27	Bristol Rovers	A	1	5
31	Colchester United	H	4	1
Feb.				
3	Crystal Palace	H	2	2
10	Northampton Town	A	0	4
17	Nottingham Forest	H	1	0
24	Ipswich Town	A	0	5
March				
3	Leicester City	H	4	3
10	Luton Town	A	1	3
17	Notts County	H	4	2
24	Mansfield Town	A	1	1
31	Peterborough United	H	3	2
April				
7				
9	Bristol Rovers	H	6	1
14	Colchester United	A	4	2
21				
28				
May				
5	Cup Final			

PROVINCIAL PRINTING & PUBLISHING CO., LTD., BUTE STREET, CARDIFF

Teams:

Cardiff City: Vearncombe; Stitfall, Milne; Hole, Rankmore, Baker; King (P), Tapscott, Ward, Durban, Pickrell.

West Ham United: Rhodes; Bond, Peters; Hurst, Brown, Moore; Musgrove, Woosnam, Seeley, Byrne, Crawford,

EXCITING DAYS IN EUROPE

The Bluebirds enjoyed mixed fortunes after being relegated from Division I. For a few years it seemed they might sink even further but under a new manager, Jimmy Scoular, matters improved to such an extent that it appeared likely a return to the top flight was once more beckoning. Among the highlights at this time were some memorable achievements against the giants of Europe in the Cup-Winners Cup.

European Cup-Winners Cup Round Two: Wednesday 23 December 1964

Cardiff City (0) 0 Sporting Lisbon (0) 0

The Football League teams in Wales changed their attitude towards the Welsh Cup when the winners were granted admission to the potentially lucrative European Cup-Winners Cup. After scraping through the first round against Esjberg of Denmark, few people expected the Bluebirds to progress any further when they were drawn against the Sporting Club of Lisbon. The previous season the Portuguese had thrashed Manchester United 5-0 on their way to winning the competition .

Astonishingly, City won the first leg in Lisbon when goals from Greg Farrell and Derek Tapscott produced a 2-1 score-line. A draw in the second leg at Ninian Park would be enough to take Cardiff through to the quarter-finals. Though it was only two days before Christmas, a passionate crowd of 25,000, by far the largest of the season, was present when the teams took the field.

It proved to be a memorable night. There were no goals but the game was filled with excitement from start to finish, and Ninian Park

The programme for the game with Sporting Lisbon shows the magnificent stadium of the Portuguese team. Even in those days Ninian Park was looking its age by comparison.

Peter Rodrigues was a fullback who used his pace to switch quickly from defence to attack. Here he brings the ball clear after breaking up a Lisbon attack.

was no place for faint hearts. After the game the Lisbon captain, Fernando Mendes, moaned about the fierce tackling by the Cardiff players. It was a view Jimmy Scoular rejected, as he pointed to the blatant Portuguese body-checking, shirt tugging and cynical fouls which left few City players without the scars of a bruising contest.

The experience of John Charles, who had signed for Cardiff for £22,500 the previous season, was vital in games such as this. After some uncertainty in the opening minutes, he and Murray, together with Rodrigues and Harrington, closed down the talented Sporting forwards with some first time tackling and excellent covering. When they did manage to penetrate the City defence, Dilwyn John provided a safe pair of hands in goal.

Not that it was one way traffic. The elegant skills of Barrie Hole created enough chances to win the game for Cardiff but Carvalho, who had given away a soft goal in

After first flattening him, Cavalho, the Portuguese goalkeeper, manhandled Derek Tapscott and removed him unceremoniously from the pitch

the first leg, was Lisbon's man of the match. Shots from Tapscott and Peter King appeared to be goal-bound until Carvalho made acrobatic saves. Charles also created havoc among Sporting's defenders when he moved up for corner kicks.

Tired limbs were forgotten by the City players as the crowd urged them on with a continual chant of "Cardiff...Cardiff". Portuguese efforts to level the tie became more desperate as the game reached its closing stages. When Carvalho tried to punch away a centre from King, he found Tapscott's chin instead. To add insult to injury, with the crowd howling, "off...off...off", Carvalho dumped him over the goal line. Tappy was soon back on the field but feelings ran even higher as Charles was flattened following a City corner. Considering the highly charged atmosphere the referee, Mr. Schaut, was handling the game well, but he missed an obvious penalty when Gomes handled a shot from Farrell on the line with Carvalho beaten.

Ten minutes from the end Don Murray brought Silva down to give away a free

JIM SCOULAR WISHES ALL CITY PATRONS A VERY HAPPY CHRISTMAS.

● A dish of Portugeese, Sir!

Jimmy Scoular, the Cardiff manager, contemplates an enjoyable Christmas after his team had disposed of Sporting Lisbon in the European Cup-winners' Cup.

kick in a dangerous position. Pinto's shot went wide of goal and in injury time it was the Bluebirds on the offensive and, perhaps appropriately, Carvalho made yet another fine save from Farrell.

At the final whistle the crowd streamed on to the pitch to mob their heroes and the Cardiff chairman, Fred Dewey, applauded the City players for "a wonderful show". Their reward was a quarter-final draw against Zaragoza of Spain. Once again they rose to the occasion in the first leg. After being 2-0 down, the team fought back to draw the match. Sadly in the return match at Ninian Park, a 40,000 crowd saw the Bluebirds go down to a 1-0 defeat. Their first European adventure was over.

Teams:
Cardiff City: John; Harrington, Rodrigues; Charles (J), Murray, Hole; Farrell, Williams, Tapscott, King, Lewis.
Sporting Lisbon: Carvalho; Gomes, Alfredo; Hilario, Mendes, Carlos; Sitoe, Silva, Figuiredo, Pinto, Morais.

Football League Division II: Tuesday 3 May 1966

Cardiff City (3) 5 Middlesbrough (2) 3

For the first time in 19 years the Bluebirds were in danger of returning to the Third Division. For Middlesbrough, in an even more precarious position, nothing short of a victory in this game would suffice if they were to avoid the drop. On the day of the match the *Echo* headline stated rather dramatically, "Survival and disaster tonight could depend on just one goal". That prophecy could not have been more wrong.

OFFICIAL **6**D. **PROGRAMME**

CARDIFF CITY
A.F.C. LTD.

Football League Division II   Tuesday, 3rd May, 1966
Kick-off 7.30 p.m.

CARDIFF CITY v MIDDLESBROUGH

The cover of the programme for the Middlesbrough match showed this photograph, taken from a recent match between the Welsh and English Grammar schools.

The match proved to be one of the most sensational ever seen at Ninian Park. City supporters were stunned when **Rooks**, the Middlesbrough centre half, headed his team into the lead from a corner. City retaliated with an all out assault on the 'Boro goal, and good combination between Peter King and Bernie Lewis gave **Barrie Hole** an opening to equalise. Knowing a draw was no use to them, Middlesbrough came back a second time. After half an hour Gareth Williams handled in the penalty area and **Rooks** scored his second goal of the evening.

Within two minutes Ian Gibson, later to play for Cardiff, committed a similar offence at the other end and **Farrell** added his name to the score sheet from the penalty spot. The crowd of just over 13,000 barely had time to catch their breath before City took the lead. **George Andrews** met a corner from Lewis and rammed the ball past Appleby. It was thrill a minute, cut and thrust football, with chances for both sides.

The drama continued in the second half. The entire City team displayed a quality and determination that had often been missing during the season but those who were there will always remember the game as "Farrell's Match". Against Middlesbrough, Greg Farrell reached heights few thought he could achieve. In this marvellously entertaining contest, he reached a level of excellence on a par with the artistry I have

Barrie Hole slides the ball past goalkeeper Appleby to level the score after Middlesbrough had taken a shock lead.

seen from wingers such as Stan Matthews, Tom Finney and even George Best. The entire 'Boro defence was at panic stations when he had the ball and Spraggon at left back came in for particular humiliation. This was the first season when substitutes were allowed but neither side changed its starting line up. It is doubtful if Spraggon would have minded if someone had taken his place.

In the 65th minute Gareth Williams found Hole just inside the Middlesbrough half, and he burst through the opposition to give **Peter King** a perfect pass for City's fourth goal. **Andrews** made the game safe with a fifth two minutes from

Greg Farrell gave a virtuoso performance against Middlesbrough. He came from Birmingham in 1964 and at times infuriated City fans with indifferent performances. Yet, on days like this, he could be brilliant.

PAGE SIXTEEN

FOOTBALL LEAGUE DIVISION II				FOOTBALL COMBINATION				WELSH LEAGUE			
1965		F.	A.	1965		F.	A.	1965		F.	A.
August				August				August			
21 Bury	H	1	0	21 Southampton	A	0	6	25 (W) Ebbw Vale	A	1	4
25 (W) Derby Co...	H	2	1	28 Tottenham H.	H	1	5				
28 Norwich City	A	2	3	September				September			
September				4 Norwich C.	A	2	1	1 (W) Bridgend	H	1	2
1 (W) Derby Co...	A	5	1	11 West Ham	H	2	2	8 (W) Abergavenny	H	1	1
4 Wolverhampton	H	1	4	18				18 Gwynfi	H	1	1
11 Rotherham Utd.	A	4	6	25 Leicester C.	H	1	5	22 (W) Merthyr	H	4	0
14 (T) Charlton A.	A	2	5	October				29 (W) Ferndale	A	1	2
18 Manchester C.	H	4	3	2 Plymouth A.	A	3	1				
25 Bristol C.	A	1	1	9 Crystal P.	H	4	5	October			
October				16 Notts Forest	A	1	1	23 Lovells Ath.	A	1	3
2 Wales v. England				20 (W) Shrewsbury	H	6	2				
at Ninian Park	0	0		23				November			
6 (W) Coventry C.	H	1	2	30 Ipswich T.	A	1	2	3 (W)			
9 Plymouth A.	A	2	2	November				20 Caerau	H	4	1
16 Portsmouth	H	1	2	6							
23 Bolton W.	A	1	2	13 Arsenal	A	1	7	December			
27 (W) Wales v. Russia				20				1 (W) Newport	A	0	2
at Ninian Park	2	1		24 (W) Chelsea	H	0	6	27 (M) Haverf'dwest	A	0	1
30 Ipswich T.	H	1	0	27 Northampton	A	0	6				
November				December				1966			
6 Birmingham C.	A	2	4	4 Notts Forest	H	2	2	January			
10 (W) Charlton A.	H	3	1	7 (Tu.) Coventry	A	0	4	8 Llanelly	H	2	1
13 (1) Leyton O.	H	3	1	11 Crystal P.	A	3	2	29 Ton Pentre	H	3	1
20 Middlesbrough	A	4	3	15 (W) Swindon	H	1	2				
27 Huddersfield T.	H	0	1	22 (W) Ipswich	H	4	4	February			
December				27				19 Bridgend	A	0	0
4 (2) Crystal P.	A	0	0								
11 Preston N.E.	A	1	3	1966				March			
18 Portsmouth	A	1	3	January				2 (W) Swansea T.	A	1	3
27 (M) Southampton	H	3	5	1 Shrewsbury T.	A	0	1	12 Caerau	A	4	1
1966 January				5 (W) Arsenal	H	2	2	19 Pembroke	H	3	3
1 Plymouth A.	H	5	1	8				23 (W) Newport	H	2	1
8 Leyton O.	A	1	1	29				26 Ferndale	H	1	2
26 (3) Port Vale (Cup)	H	2	1	February				30 (W) Abergavenny	A	0	4
29 Bury	A	1	1	5 Tottenham	A	2	5				
February				12 Peterborough	H	1	5	April			
12 (4) Southport (Cup)	A	0	2	16 (W) South'ton	H	2	1	6 (W) Llanelly	A	0	1
19 Wolverhampton	A	1	2	19				18 (M) South Wales			
26 Rotherham U.	H	0	0	23 (W) Norwich	H	0	0	Switchgear	H	5	3
March				March				20 (W) Swansea T.	H	1	1
5 (5) Bolton W.	H	1	1	5 Peterborough	A	2	4	25 (M) Haverf'dwest	H	1	1
12 Man. City	A	2	2	9 (W) Coventry	H	1	1	30 South Wales			
18 (F) Bristol City	H	2	1	12				Switchgear..	A		
26 (6) Coventry C.	A	1	3	April							
April				2 Chelsea	A	1	6	May			
2 Birmingham C.	H	1	3	9 Northampton	H	3	3	2 (M) Ton Pentre	A		
8 (F) Carlisle Utd.	H	1	1	16							
9 Ipswich T.	A	1	2	23 Fulham	A	3	4	(M)—Monday			
12 (T) Carlisle Utd.	A	0	2	27 (W) Plymouth	H	2	3	(T)—Tuesday			
20 (W) Southampton	A	2	3	30				(W)—Wednesday			
23 (S.F.) Huddersfield	A	1	1	May				(F)—Friday			
30 Crystal P.	H			4 (W) Fulham	H						
May				7 West Ham	A						
4 (T) Middlesbrough	H										
7 Preston N.E.	A										
10 (T) Norwich C.	H										
14 (FINAL)											

Copyright of the Football League Ltd., 1965

Provincial Printing and Publishing Co., Ltd., Ferry Road, Cardiff

Cardiff's results for the 1965-66 season indicate why the game with Middlesbrough was a make or break affair.

time. Inevitably the man who created it for him was Farrell. There was just time for **Rooks** to complete his hat trick when he drove home a free kick from 20 yards. It must be unusual if not unique for a centre half to score a hat trick and still finish on the losing team. The only blight on Cardiff's evening was a nasty injury to Gareth Williams's right knee.

The result sent Middlesbrough into the Third Division for the first time in their history while the Bluebirds lived to fight another day. Manager Jimmy Scoular praised their performance: "I couldn't have asked more from them last night". What he said after City's final two games is unknown and almost certainly unprintable. Their outstanding form against Middlesbrough deserted them afterwards. On Saturday Cardiff suffered the humiliation of a 9-0 thrashing at Preston and the following Tuesday the crowd, which had cheered the players to the echo a week earlier, booed them off the field when the Bluebirds lost their last home game 2-0 to Norwich.

Teams:

Cardiff City: John; Coldrick, Carver; Williams (G), Murray, Hole; Farrell, Ferguson, Andrews, King, Lewis; Johnston (sub not used).

Middlesbrough: Appleby; Butler, Spraggon; Horner, Rooks, Davidson; Downing, Gibson, Irvine, McMordie, Jones.

European Cup-Winners Cup Semi-final: 1 May 1968

Cardiff City (1) 2 HSV Hamburg (1) 3

By 1968 Jimmy Scoular had almost completed the rebuilding of the Cardiff City team after spending the previous two seasons fighting relegation. Shrewd signings such as Brian Clark, Barrie Jones, Brian Harris and Les Lea were added to the home grown talents of John Toshack, Peter King and Don Murray. The result was a side which could not only compete in Division II but also won admiration in Europe.

The run in the Cup-Winners Cup began with comfortable victories against Shamrock Rovers and NAC Breda but then the Bluebirds drew the formidable Russian side, Moscow Torpedo. The tie evoked memories of the game with Dynamo in 1945 but there was to be no repeat of that fiasco. After home and away legs, the teams were level on aggregate at 1-1. There was no penalty shoot-out in those days but Norman Dean's goal in a play-off at Augsburg was enough to take Cardiff into the semi-final.

The first leg was played in Hamburg before 70,000 fanatical Germans and City fought a magnificent rearguard action to come away with a 1-1 draw. The players received a rapturous reception when they returned to Cardiff Airport, and hopes were high that they would finish the job at Ninian Park to reach the final.

Peter Jackson in the *South Wales Echo* forecast, "a battle of titanic proportion", a view shared among the crowd of 43,000. Brian Clark, who had been a consistent goal scorer since Scoular signed him from Bristol City, was ineligible for selection. His place was taken by Norman Dean who had scored vital goals both against Torpedo and in the first leg with Hamburg. The HSV team contained four German internationals though Willi Schultz, who had been capped 49 times for his country, was injured and his place was taken by Holger Dieckmann.

After seven minutes **Dean** justified his selection by giving Cardiff the perfect start. Lea and King combined well and, when the ball was crossed, he swept it past Ankos Oezcan, Hamburg's

CARDIFF CITY	v.	H.S.V. HAMBURG
(Royal Blue and White)		(White and Red)
Bobby WILSON	1	Ankos OEZCAN
David CARVER	2	Helmut SANDMANN
Bobby FERGUSON	3	Juergen KURBJUHN
Norman DEAN	4	Klaus HELLFITZ
Don MURRAY	5	Egon HORST
Brian HARRIS	6	W̶i̶l̶i̶ ̶S̶C̶H̶U̶L̶Z̶ Hol
Barrie JONES	7	Hans SCHULZ Dieck
Malcolm CLARKE	8	Werner KRAEMER
Peter KING	9	Uwe SEELER
John TOSHACK	10	Franz-Josef HOENIG
Leslie LEA	11	Gert DOERFEL
Lyn DAVIES	12	Erhard SCHWERIN

Referee:
Mr. L. van RAVENS
(Netherlands)

Linesmen:
Mr. A. P. BOM, (Netherlands)
(Red Flag)
Mr. A. van GEMERT, (Netherlands)
(Yellow Flag)

THE ROATH FURNISHING COMPANY

How the teams lined up for the Cup-winners semi-final between Cardiff and HSV Hamburg. Among Hamburg's international stars was Uwe Seeler who had played against England in the 1966 World Cup Final.

The Hamburg goalkeeper, Turkish international Ankos Oezcan, saves a shot from Peter King, one of several chances missed by the City in the first half.

Turkish goalkeeper. The Germans were level ten minutes later when Seeler was able to centre to **Hoenig** whose shot gave Bob Wilson no chance. From that moment until half-time Cardiff dominated the game, but Lea missed two open goals and Oezcan made three spectacular saves.

The Bluebirds were made to regret those missed chances 11 minutes after half-time. Wilson was off his line when **Seeler** sent a harmless lob towards goal which dipped just under the bar. For a time the Germans appeared likely to increase their lead

Hamburg always posed a threat with set pieces. Nine City players line up to defend this free kick in the first half.

but, urged on by the crowd, City stormed back for a grandstand finish. With a quarter of an hour to go, Barrie Jones was fouled on the edge of the Hamburg penalty area. He took the free kick and, from a pin-point cross, **Brian Harris** headed an equaliser. In their excitement fans invaded the pitch and, in the extra time added for the stoppage, there was one final twist. With both sides apparently reconciled to a play-off in Jutland, **Hoenig** put in a harmless looking shot from 30 yards. Wilson appeared to have it covered but it rolled off his jersey into the net. It was a heart-breaking end to a wonderful cup-tie.

The *Echo* headline summed up the feelings of City fans, "Glory run ends in tragedy and tears". Wilson was understandably distraught, yet his heroic displays against Moscow Torpedo and in the first leg against Hamburg had been instrumental in taking Cardiff so far in the competition. Scoular believed his side was worth at least a replay and even Uwe Seeler admitted Hamburg were lucky.

For most of the game, Cardiff had been on top, playing with a skill and style that had not been seen at Ninian Park for many years. All the City team played well but Brian Harris captained the side superbly, displaying all the class that marked his distinguished career with Everton. Hamburg went on to lose 2-0 to Milan in the final. For Cardiff it was the end of a great adventure in which the team had brought pride to themselves and to British football.

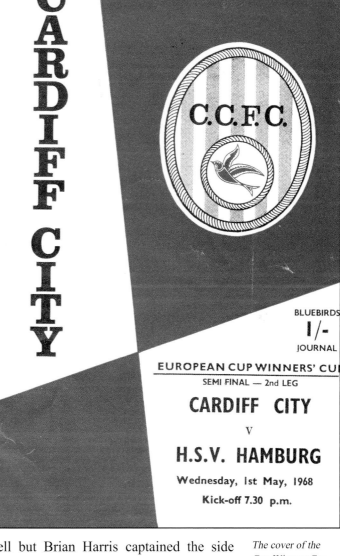

The cover of the Cup Winners Cup semi-final programme. The Bluebirds came so close to reaching a European final in this match with Hamburg.

Football League Division II: Saturday 31 October 1970

Cardiff City (2) 5 Hull City (1) 1

For a third successive season, Cardiff City were challenging for promotion to the First Division. Hopes were high that this would be the Bluebirds' year as they made a good start to the season and were well equipped for a promotion challenge. The linch-pin in defence was Don Murray, one of the finest centre halves to represent the club. A hard tackling defender, Murray played 483 times for Cardiff and in 1970 he was at the peak

Ian Gibson in action against Hull. His ability to hold the ball and control the midfield set up goal-scoring opportunities for other players.

of his career. Before the season began Jimmy Scoular acquired a skilful midfield general when he signed Ian Gibson for £35,000 from Coventry. Leading the attack was John Toshack, now among the most prolific goal-scorers in Division II. Still only 21, he was fulfilling the potential he had first revealed when, at the age of 16, he had scored in his first game for Cardiff.

The game with Hull promised to be closely contested as they too were enjoying a good season and came to Ninian Park as League leaders. Their success was based on a mean defence which had conceded only nine goals in 14 matches. On a damp afternoon, before a crowd of nearly 22,000, that record was demolished by a rampant Cardiff team and an unforgettable display by Toshack.

John Toshack turns away in triumph as he scores his first goal against Hull. Few among the spectators realised John was making his last appearance for the Bluebirds at Ninian Park.

The fans did not have long to wait for the first goal. After six minutes a cross to the far post from Gary Bell allowed **Toshack** to out-jump the Hull defenders and head past McKechnie. Ten minutes later Murray made a powerful run down the right and from his centre **Toshack** scored his second goal of the afternoon. A shell-shocked Hull tried to rally and, when **Barker** headed home a free kick, the game was once more in the balance.

Cardiff continued to dominate and in the 59th minute Toshack and Woodruff exchanged passes before **Toshack** completed his hat-trick with a thunderous left foot volley into the roof of the net. The big striker acknowledged the plaudits of the crowd with his arm raised in triumph. Hull were now a well beaten side, and Toshack became the goal provider when he flicked on a corner from King to **Gibson** for goal number four. Seven minutes from time **Leighton Phillips** completed the scoring with a 25 yard shot which bounced off the unfortunate McKechnie's chest into the net.

"Toshack tears in to tame the Tigers" was the *Football Echo* headline. It was a

Bobby Woodruff almost adds another goal for the City as Hull's goalkeeper, Ian McKechnie, dives to make a fine save.

superb display by the City and Toshack's hat-trick underlined the key role he was playing in the team. Such performances were bound to attract interest from the giants of the First Division and Liverpool, one of the leading clubs in the country, had been tracking him for some time. When Bill Shankly made a bid for his services, the City directors argued they could not stand in Toshack's way.

While the move to Liverpool was great for Toshack, City supporters believed it showed a deplorable lack of ambition within the club. It was certainly a turning point in Cardiff's season. The Bluebirds were in no hurry to sign a replacement and, in the

Cardiff received £110,000 when John Toshack was transferred to Liverpool. Their manager, Bill Shankly commented, "He'd be cheap at a million".

next seven games, the team picked up only six points. Toshack's replacement, Alan Warboys, was finally signed from Sheffield Wednesday six weeks after his departure. With 13 goals in 17 matches, Warboys set Cardiff on the promotion trail once more but the loss of momentum while City were trying to sign him, proved crucial at the end of the season. Eventually the City finished in third place, three points behind Sheffield United, and in those days only the top two teams were promoted.

Teams:
Cardiff City: Eadie; Carver, Bell, Sutton, Murray, Harris, Gibson, Toshack, Phillips, Woodruff, King; Clark (sub. not used)
Hull City: McKechnie; Beardsley, de Vries, Wilkinson, Neill, Simpkin, Jarvis, Houghton, Pearson, Wagstaff, Barker (sub. Butler).

European Cup-Winners Cup Quarter-final: Wednesday 10 March 1971

Cardiff City 1 (1) Real Madrid 0 (0)

"Plum European draw for City" was how the *South Wales Echo* placards described the Bluebirds' quarter-final tie with Real Madrid, when the draw was made in Paris. Real had won the European Cup six times and were the most famous club team in the world. The side included six of the side that had won the European Cup in 1966 but they were an ageing team in decline, and definitely not the power they had been in the previous 15 years.

The Bluebirds could not have asked for a more glamorous match when they drew Real Madrid in the quarter –finals of the Cup Winners Cup. This is how the club advertised its ticket sales.

CARDIFF CITY v REAL MADRID

European Cup Winners Cup Tie (Home Leg)
at NINIAN PARK, CARDIFF
on Wednesday, March 10, 1971. K.O. 7.30pm
Ground tickets available at 40p, all stand and enclosure tickets sold. This is an all ticket match, please come early to avoid the rush

In reaching the quarter-finals, Cardiff had hammered Larnaca from Cyprus 8-0 and followed that result with a 7-2 aggregate win over Nantes, Cardiff's twin city. The Bluebirds' confidence was high going into the match. They were still well in the running for promotion and the previous Saturday had thrashed Carlisle 4-0, all the goals coming from Alan Warboys who was not eligible for this match.

Before the game City had another worry as Nigel Rees, their 17 year old winger, was wanted by Wales for a UEFA Youth cup-tie against Scotland. Fortunately, common sense prevailed and the Welsh FA realised that Rees would benefit more from the encounter with Real. As events proved, his inclusion was to be crucial to the outcome of the match.

These were the teams for the game with Real. The Bluebirds were without Alan Warboys who was signed too late to play in the match.

Real were lying third in the Spanish League and had won five and drawn one of their last six games. The official attendance for the match was 47,500 but it is likely that at least 2,000 more people found a way into Ninian Park for what was to prove an unforgettable night. It was clear from the outset that the Spaniards had come to defend, though the Bluebirds had a lucky escape after five minutes when Dave Carver's back pass was intercepted by Perez. He had a clear shot at goal but, fortunately for the City, he shot straight at Jim Eadie. After that the City goalkeeper had little to do.

It was not long before Cardiff began to control the match. In the 32nd minute Gary Bell began a move by releasing the ball down the line to Bobby Woodruff. After beating one opponent he passed to Nigel Rees. Confronted by two defenders, the youngster seemed to have lost the ball, but it bounced in his favour and he launched a superb cross from the left. An unmarked **Brian Clar**k met it with his head to give Cardiff the lead.

As the match went on, City should have scored more goals but 1-0 was how it finished. Would it be enough with the away leg in Madrid still to come? For the moment no-one cared as the *Echo* reporter wrote: "Whatever happens in Madrid, nobody can take anything away from the players for their wonderful show last night."

TONIGHT'S LINE UP

CARDIFF CITY (Royal Blue, White)	v.		REAL MADRID (All white)
Jim EADIE	1		BORJA
David CARVER	2		GRANDE
Gary BELL	3		SANCHIS
Mel SUTTON	4		ZOCO
Don MURRAY	5		ZUNZUNEGUI
Leighton PHILLIPS	6		BENITO
Ian GIBSON	7		AMANCIO
Brian CLARK	8		PIRRI
Peter KING	9		GROSSO
John PARSONS	10		VELAZQUEZ
Nigel REES	11		PEREZ
Bobby WOODRUFF	12		JUNQUERA

Referee:
VITAL LORAUX
(Belgium)

THE ROATH FURNISHING COMPANY

Linesmen:
LEON GIJSELINCK, (Belgium)
(Yellow flag)

JEAN PAUL BINST, (Belgium)
(Red flag)

After scoring the winner against Real Madrid, Brian Clark said: "No goal has ever given me greater pleasure and I don't suppose I'll ever get one to please me so much again".

Brian Clark was the man of the hour but typically his first response after scoring was to congratulate Nigel Rees on the cross that led to it. In his autobiography, Brian Clark mentions how often fans reminisce with him about that night when he scored the goal that beat Real Madrid. On 10 March 2006 the eleven that played in that match were re-united for a charity dinner.

The second leg was played two weeks later in Madrid. In a bad-tempered game the Czech referee was intimidated by the home crowd. Apart from giving Real 35 free kicks to Cardiff's six, he did nothing to protect the City players from a hostile crowd. Beer cans were hurled on to the pitch and Gary Bell was hit by a flying bottle. Later a Spanish journalist excused the crowd's reaction with the comment: "What do you British expect when you won't let us Spanish have Gibraltar"? Until half-time the Bluebirds held their own but the tie was settled in two minutes early in the second half when defensive lapses resulted in two Real goals. So the Spaniards won 2-1 on aggregate and City's European dream was over.

In those days, winning the Welsh Cup with its entry into Europe seemed a formality for the Bluebirds but, while they competed in the Cup-Winners' competition several more times, they achieved little success. In 1994 UEFA restricted Welsh access to its competitions to clubs playing in the Welsh League. Nor, as a Welsh club, could Cardiff qualify for European football through the English League system. A change of heart took place in 2008 when the Bluebirds reached the FA Cup Final and the Football Association ruled that, if the Bluebirds had won the Cup, they would have been eligible for entry into the UEFA Cup.

One of Jimmy Scoular's best moves in the transfer market was the acquisition of Brian Clark from Huddersfield for £8,000. In two spells with the City, he scored over 100 goals for the club.

City met with a hostile reception in the return match in Madrid. Leighton Phillips and Don Murray show the referee a broken bottle thrown at Gary Bell.

With two points for a win and one for a draw, the league table before the match with Crystal Palace shows how crucial the game was for both sides.

HOW WE STAND . . . DIVISION II

			Home					Away					
	P	W	D	L	For	Agst		W	D	L	For	Agst	Pts
1. Middlesbrough	42	16	4	1	40	8		11	7	3	37	22	65
2. Luton Town	41	12	5	3	39	21		7	7	7	22	26	50
3. Carlisle United	42	13	5	3	40	17		7	4	10	21	31	49
4. Blackpool	42	11	5	5	35	17		6	8	7	22	23	47
5. Orient	41	9	7	4	27	16		6	10	5	27	25	47
6. Nottingham Forest	42	12	6	3	40	19		3	9	9	17	24	45
7. Sunderland	41	11	6	4	32	15		7	3	10	22	26	45
8. West Bromwich Albion	42	8	9	4	28	24		6	7	8	20	21	44
9 Hull City	42	9	9	3	25	15		4	8	9	21	32	43
10. Notts County	42	8	6	7	30	35		7	7	7	25	25	43
11. Bolton Wanderers	42	12	5	4	30	17		3	7	11	14	23	42
12. Millwall	42	10	6	5	28	16		4	8	9	23	35	42
13. Fulham	42	11	4	6	26	20		5	6	10	13	23	42
14. Aston Villa	41	8	9	4	33	21		5	5	10	14	23	40
15. Portsmouth	42	9	8	4	26	16		5	4	12	19	46	40
16. Bristol City	42	9	5	7	25	20		5	5	11	22	34	38
17. Oxford United	42	8	8	5	27	21		2	8	11	8	25	36
18. Sheffield Wednesday	42	9	6	6	33	24		3	5	13	18	39	35
19. Cardiff City	**41**	**8**	**6**	**6**	**26**	**19**		**2**	**9**	**10**	**22**	**42**	**35**
20. Crystal Palace	41	6	7	8	24	24		5	4	11	18	31	33
21. Preston North End	42	7	8	6	24	23		2	6	13	16	39	31
22. Swindon Town	42	6	7	8	22	27		1	4	16	14	45	25

An excellent equalising goal by Tony Villars against Crystal Palace was enough to give City another season in Division II.

UPS AND DOWNS OF DIVISIONS II AND III

After failing to gain promotion in 1971, the Bluebirds entered into a period of decline. Twice they were relegated to Division III but on each occasion they achieved immediate promotion back to the Second Division. Any hopes of building on success were hampered by a lack of investment, though money was found for ground improvements, some of them essential. Two new wings were added to the Grandstand in 1973 to increase its capacity to 3,300 but in 1977 the Grangetown Stand was demolished for safety reasons.

How the teams lined up for the relegation battle. The referee, Jack Taylor, took charge of the World Cup Final between West Germany and Holland a few months later.

Football League Division II: Tuesday 30 April 1974

Cardiff City (1) 1 Crystal Palace (1) 1

For a third successive season, Cardiff City faced a relegation battle. In 1972 the Bluebirds had missed the drop by one point and a year later they had an even closer shave, when only a superior goal average secured their Second Division status. In November 1973 Jimmy Scoular paid the price of the team's failure and was sacked. Frank O'Farrell was chosen as the new manager but the season was ending with another desperate battle to avoid relegation.

This was the season in which the Football League introduced its policy of three up and three down in each of its divisions. In the Second Division, Preston and Swindon were already relegated and either Crystal Palace or Cardiff would join them at the end of this match. The issue was a simple one. City needed a draw to avoid going down and Palace had to win. Ironically this nerve racking finale occurred because the fixture had been re-arranged after a waterlogged pitch prevented the teams from playing on the scheduled date in February.

A crowd of nearly 27,000, including many Palace supporters, saw a tense, nail biting game. After 29 minutes City supporters feared the worst as Palace took the lead. Ron Healey vainly appealed that he had been fouled, as an in-swinging corner from Peter Taylor led to a scramble on the goal-line and **Stewart Jump** forced the ball into the net. The visitors now took control of the game, playing with a confidence that belied their lowly League position.

It was Tony Villars who lifted the gloom among Cardiff supporters with a splendid goal after 39 minutes. He began the move in his own half, beating two opponents before he was tackled on the edge of the Palace penalty area. He managed to push a pass to Gil Reece, who cleverly shielded the ball, and guided it into an open space for **Villars** to unleash a powerful shot past goalkeeper Paul Hammond.

Knowing a draw would be enough to save them from relegation, the whole team played with a commitment that had been lacking in recent weeks. In the second half it was largely a rearguard action as Palace piled on the pressure and missed several goal-scoring opportunities. Blyth should certainly have scored when confronted with an open goal, while Healey made a magnificent save from Taylor. Opportunities for the City forwards were limited and came mainly from the skills of Villars who had an outstanding game. Bluebird supporters anxiously counted down the minutes to the final whistle and when it came their cheers were as much from relief as from joy.

It was the final game for Frank O'Farrell who was leaving to become manager of the Iranian national team. It was confirmed after the match that assistant coach, Jimmy Andrews, would take his place. For the third successive year, the Bluebirds had just held on to their Second Division status but, amid the relief and euphoria that followed the game, Andrews made it clear there was little money available to strengthen the team. A year later their luck ran out and after 28 years Cardiff City returned to Division III.

Football League Division III: Wednesday 14 April 1976

Cardiff City (0) 2 Hereford United (0) 0

After the Bluebirds were relegated in 1975, changes took place in the boardroom at Ninian Park and there was an optimistic air as the new directors made cash available

Tony Evans (left) and Adrian Alston scored 35 goals in the 1975-76 season. They were major contributors to City's successful promotion campaign.

to strengthen the team. Jimmy Andrews showed excellent judgement in finding the players who would take the City back to Division II at the first attempt.

Mike England, who had enjoyed a distinguished career at centre half for Tottenham and Wales, was persuaded to postpone his retirement. To add strength to the forward line, Tony Evans, who had failed to make an impression at Blackpool, was signed on a free transfer. In November, Andrews found him a partner as he paid £20,000 for the Australian international, Adrian Alston, and these two became the spearhead of the attack. The signing of Doug Livermore

from Norwich for £20,000 gave additional support to the midfield skills of John Buchanan and Willie Anderson.

Hereford United were enjoying the best season in their history, and the team owed that success mainly to the free-scoring duo of Dixie McNeil and Steve Davey who had scored 49 goals between them. The Bulls came to Ninian Park virtually certain of winning the Third Division Championship, but the fight for the other two promotion places was still being fought out among Cardiff, Millwall, Brighton and Crystal Palace.

Ron Healey was well beaten by this header from John Layton in the first half of the game with Hereford but the referee had already blown his whistle for offside

A few weeks earlier Hereford had defeated the City 4-1 at Edgar Street so the Bluebirds were looking for revenge. With so much at stake, there were few scoring opportunities for either side in the first half, as tension gripped the players and the game was disrupted by a series of niggling fouls. Peter Sayer had a golden opportunity to put Cardiff ahead after five minutes but managed to hit his shot across goal and into touch. John Layton did put the ball in the net for Hereford but the linesman's flag was already up for offside.

The second half proved to be much more exciting. In the 54th minute a pass from Freddie Pethard sent Evans racing down the left wing. His centre was met by **Livermore** who headed Cardiff into the lead. The Bluebirds were now on top and, in an attempt to add more fire to their attack, the visitors replaced Terry Paine with a third striker, Eric Redrobe. The game developed into a fiery encounter as Galley was booked for a heavy tackle on Alston and Sayer was forced to retire with a leg injury. Three minutes from time Alan Campbell, who had joined Cardiff from Birmingham a few weeks earlier, made certain of the points. Again Evans began the move with a pass to Livermore who crossed the ball to **Campbell.** Coolly he rounded the goalkeeper before tapping it into the net for his solitary goal of the season.

Kevin Charlton is beaten as Doug Livermore scores City's first goal against Hereford. Steve Ritchie can only watch helplessly

Four days before the game with Hereford, City had produced an outstanding display at Selhurst Park to defeat Crystal Palace. The colourful Palace manager, Malcolm Allison, who had done a great deal of boasting before the match, afterwards claimed Cardiff would never match the crowd of 25,863 that had seen the game. In fact a crowd of 35,459, the largest since the game against Tottenham in 1961, assembled to witness this gripping encounter with Hereford. Just to remind Allison of his comments, the club sent him six bottles of champagne with the message, "With love from Cardiff City".

Gil Reece is challenged by Roy Carter (left) and Dudley Tyler as he uses his pace to burst through the Hereford defence.

Hereford's manager, John Sillett, generously admitted Cardiff were the better side on the night. The two sides met again a few weeks later when the Bluebirds triumphed again to win the Welsh Cup. Cardiff clinched promotion in their final match at Bury but, unfortunately, key players such as Anderson, Livermore, Alston and Mike England, who was later to coach the Welsh team, all left within a year. For six years the Bluebirds faced an uphill battle in clinging tenaciously to their Second Division status.

Teams:
Cardiff City: Healey; Dwyer, Pethard, Campbell, England; Lamour, Sayer (sub. Reece), Livermore; Evans, Alston, Anderson.
Hereford United: Charlton; Emery, Ritchie, Layton, Galley; Lindsay, Paine (sub. Redrobe), Tyler; Davey, McNeil, Carter.

FA Cup Round Three: Saturday 8 January 1977

Cardiff City (1) 1 Tottenham Hotspur (0) 0

When the Bluebirds drew Tottenham in the third round of the Cup, Jimmy Andrews described the tie as "a dream of a draw". Though Spurs were languishing near the foot of the First Division, they were still an attractive team and the crowd of 27,868 was by far the largest of the season.

Robin Friday, City's new signing from Reading, was cup-tied so Peter Sayer was playing as an emergency striker. He gave Cardiff the perfect start with a sensational goal. The move began when Ralph Coates mistimed his header just inside his own half and the ball fell to Steve Grapes who quickly passed it to **Sayer**. One of the fastest players in the game, he outpaced the Tottenham defence and fired a shot past Jennings from more than 20 yards to score a brilliant goal. It was only his third in 53 matches but, as he said afterwards, it was, "a moment of magic that I shall remember for the rest of my life".

While the early goal lifted the City team, Tottenham soon responded and Glenn Hoddle, still a newcomer in the side, began to show the technique and

For the cup-tie with Tottenham, Cardiff issued a souvenir programme. The cover is not very exciting but inside were memories of some great encounters from the past between these two sides.

Cardiff City
(Blue with Yellow, White stripe)
1   Ron HEALEY
2   Phil DWYER
3   Clive CHARLES
4   John BUCHANAN
5   Paul WENT
6   Albert LARMOUR
7   Steve GRAPES
8   Doug LIVERMORE
9   Tony EVANS
10 Brian ATTLEY
11 Peter SAYER
12

Tottenham Hotspur
(White shirts, Blue shorts)
Pat JENNINGS   1
Terry TAYLOR   2
John GORMAN   3
Glenn HODDLE   4
John PRATT   5
Keith OSGOOD   6
Alfie CONN   7
Steve PERRYMAN   8
John DUNCAN   9
Ralph COATES   10
Peter TAYLOR   11
12

Referee:
A. LEES (Bridgwater)
Linesmen:
K. BISSIX
(Red Flag)
W. M. BROMBROFF
(Yellow Flag)

THE **ROATH** FURNISHING COMPANY

Todays match ball donated by
PROVINCIAL PRINTING &
PUBLISHING COMPANY LTD.

A great moment for David Giles. City's substitute against Hereford United hooks this right foot shot clear of Kevin Charlton for the so-important opening goal. "Yes, it gave me a tremendous lift," says the Wales Youth international who is impatient for first team football.
Picture by kind permission of the Football Echo

This was the team sheet for the match with Spurs. In their side were Pat Jennings, still one of the finest goalkeepers in Britain, and Glenn Hoddle, just beginning his distinguished career.

silky skills that would later make him one of the greatest talents in English football. Yet a magnificent City defence allowed the visitors few clear chances.

In the second half Spurs continued to press for an equalising goal but at the expense of leaving gaps in their defence. When Sayer and Tony Evans were able to break, they went close to adding the second goal that would have eased the tension. As the game moved into its final stages, the Bluebirds were intent on preserving their

Peter Sayer's goal against Tottenham impressed the BBC so much that it became a regular feature for the rest of the season in Match of the Day.

lead and, in a storming Spurs' finale, Taylor twice came close to levelling the score. First a 20 yard shot was deflected, almost sending Healey the wrong way and a few minutes later the same player hit the post and the ball cannoned back into Healey's arms. As the final whistle blew, the crowd rose to salute what had been a magnificent team effort.

While Sayer's wonder goal was the talking point after the match, it was the City defenders who took the honours as the game progressed. When the Tottenham forwards reached the Cardiff penalty area, they found a Welsh iron curtain in front of them. Healey and Attley played well while Paul Went and Phil Dwyer were outstanding. Went enjoyed his best game since joining Cardiff from Portsmouth, while the *Western Mail* reporter claimed that some of Dwyer's clearances had, "the quality of a bionic man".

Glenn Hoddle leaps for the ball but Ron Healey gathers safely in the cup-tie with Spurs. Paul Went watches anxiously.

The reward for the Bluebirds' success was a home tie with Wrexham, then enjoying the most successful period in their history. The game proved to be another thriller, as Wrexham fought back to equalise after being two goals down. With time running out, John Buchanan scored a superb individual goal to put City in the fifth round. Again the Bluebirds were drawn at home to Everton and fans began to wonder how far the City might progress in the competition. Tony Evans gave Cardiff an early lead but it was the First Division team that finally came out on top by two goals to one.

The cup run was the highlight of a disappointing season, as Cardiff only just avoided returning to Division III after a desperate 1-1 draw with Carlisle in the last game. Tottenham's season ended with relegation from the First Division and in September the two teams met again at Ninian Park in a League match. This time it was the Spurs who came out on top with a 1-0 victory.

Football League Division II: Saturday 27 December 1980

Cardiff City (1) 3 Swansea City (2) 3

This was probably the most dramatic match ever played at Ninian Park between these two great rivals. There was an added spice to the encounter as John Toshack, once such a great favourite at Ninian Park, was managing Swansea and managing them very successfully. When he left Liverpool in 1978 he hoped to make a return to his

The cover of the match programme for Cardiff's dramatic match with Swansea. The action picture is taken from an earlier game with Wrexham.

native Cardiff. Instead the club spurned his services and the Swans became the lucky beneficiaries. As their player-manager, he had taken the team from the Fourth Division to the Second in successive seasons, and now his side was challenging for promotion to Division I. Had he come to Cardiff as he wished, the future of the club could have been transformed.

The Bluebirds were very much the underdogs for this game, despite an unbeaten run in their last six matches. Toshack had spent a million pounds building up a talented squad. It included ex-Cardiff City players, Brian Attley and Leighton Phillips, as well as Welsh internationals Leighton James, John Mahoney, Alan Curtis and Robbie James. Another of his star signings was the Yugoslav defender, Dzemal Hadziabdic.

The crowd of 21,239 included thousands of Swansea supporters in confident mood. However, it was the Bluebirds who struck first after 12 minutes. John

It was first blood to the Bluebirds against Swansea as Gary Stevens gave them an early lead with a shot from close range.

The Swans' goalkeeper, Dave Stewart, safely gathers the ball as Peter Kitchen rushes in to make a determined challenge.

Buchanan hit a perfect pass from 40 yards to **Gary Stevens** whose close range goal ended a run of 21 games without scoring. The quality of Swansea's football showed why they were among the high flyers in the division, but City seemed to have few problems in containing them. Then, in the 40th minute, Phil Dwyer gave away possession with a poor pass, and Brian Attley was able to slip the ball to **Neil Robinson** to equalise for Swansea. Three minutes later Healey failed to hold a powerful drive from Robbie James and **Alan Curtis** fastened on to the rebound to give the Swans a 2-1 lead at the interval.

In the second half Dwyer, who was suffering from a thigh injury, was replaced by Paul Giles and, even though the Bluebirds were forced to reorganise their defence, they pressed hard for an equalising goal. Their efforts seemed to be in vain 17 minutes from the end, when an unmarked **Leighton James** headed Swansea's third goal. City refused to give up but, five minutes from the end, Cardiff supporters began to drift out of the ground. Those unfortunates missed a tremendous climax to the game. With two minutes left, a feeble back pass from Nigel Stephenson allowed **Peter Kitchen** to nip in and make it 3-2.

John Buchanan's equaliser against Swansea was one of the finest goals ever scored at Ninian Park. He began the game with seven stitches in his foot but afterwards said, "I have never struck a shot better in my entire career".

Just a few seconds remained on the clock when Cardiff were awarded a free kick at the Grange end more than 35 yards from the Swansea goal. Wayne Hughes touched the ball to **John Buchanan** who unleashed a thunderous volley that left David Stewart helpless. Toshack could not believe his eyes: "I have never seen a goal like it. I was hoping Buchanan would shoot because you cannot score from that range". Had the match been televised it would almost certainly have won the "goal of the season" competition.

Buchanan was renowned for his powerful shooting and scored 61 goals in 264 games for the City. The thunderbolt against Swansea was the most spectacular of them all.

As it was, it gave the City an honourable draw. It was a result the team deserved even though Swansea were undeniably the more skilful side. Toshack was generous to his old team, expressing his admiration of the way they battled away, "even when they were on the floor". At the same time he was disappointed that his team had surrendered a two goal advantage. Later, he wrote in his autobiography how much he wanted to beat Cardiff that day to show them the mistake they had made in rejecting him three years earlier.

The return match at the Vetch Field was also drawn. The Bluebirds just managed to avoid relegation that season but it was only a temporary reprieve, and a year later they once more descended into the Third Division. Toshack became a hero in Swansea as his team gained promotion to the First Division in the last game of the season. The Swans survived for two years in the top flight before they were relegated, and began a slide that was as spectacular as its rise. Inevitably Toshack was made the scapegoat for their decline and took his managerial talents abroad.

Teams:
Cardiff City: Healey; Jones, Lewis, Pontin, Dwyer (sub. Giles), Bishop, Kitchen, Stevens, Ronson, Buchanan.
Swansea City: Stewart; Attley, Hadziabdic, Mahoney, Stephenson, Phillips, Curtis, James (R), James (L), Charles, Robinson; Rushbury (sub. not used)

Football League Division III: Saturday 7 May 1983

Cardiff City (1) 2 Leyton Orient (0) 0

When Len Ashurst became Cardiff's manager in March 1982, his appointment arrived too late to save the club from relegation, but in the close season he built a team which was capable of challenging for an immediate return to Division II. Among his new signings were Paul Bodin, Jeff Hemmerman, David Tong and Roger Gibbins, all of them free transfers. Ashurst paid a modest £10,000 for Jimmy Mullen, who proved to be a tower of strength in defence, and in November 1982 he signed Bob Hatton, 35 years old but a proven goal scorer. These newcomers, together with talented players already at the club, particularly Dave Bennett and his brother Gary, turned Cardiff into a formidable Third Division team.

Phil Dwyer is one of Cardiff City's legends. He played a record 573 times for the club over a period of 14 years.

Of the veterans no-one played a bigger part in the team's success than Phil Dwyer. "Joe", as he was better known, was not a natural footballer. He lacked pace and was not the most skilful of players, but his indomitable spirit and uncompromising defending made him a firm favourite at Ninian Park. He was now approaching the end of his career but these qualities were never better displayed than during this season.

The Bluebirds' form had dipped in March and, following a 1-0 defeat at Newport on Easter Monday, it seemed their promotion chances were fading. The team rallied and won four of the next five matches. One point

Bob Hatton fires in a low ground shot against Leyton Orient. His nine goals in 29 appearances helped City to win promotion.

from this match with Orient would be enough to guarantee promotion. Considering the importance of the occasion, the crowd of 11,480 was disappointing. Len Ashurst philosophically commented: "People aren't interested in Third Division soccer at Ninian Park and I don't blame them for that, because they should never have had it".

The match was no classic and City seemed to be suffering from nerves, as the team laboured to overcome a poor Orient side that included Peter Kitchen who had left

As a successful season draws to its close, Dave Bennett (left) and John Lewis celebrate the Bluebirds' return to Division II.

Cardiff two years earlier. The Londoners were fighting to avoid relegation and their problems increased when they were reduced to ten men. David Peach, who had already been booked, was sent off for a foul on Linden Jones. Just before half-time Cardiff broke the deadlock with a controversial goal. In a scramble in the City goal mouth, Peter Smith headed for goal and the ball appeared to hit Gibbins' arm. Appeals for a penalty went unheeded and, when play moved to the other end, Hemmerman appeared to be offside before he passed to **John Lewis** to open the score.

There could be no argument about the second goal. When **Dave Bennett** received the ball from Hemmerman, he beat two defenders before hitting a low shot past Mervyn Day. As the game ended, the crowd invaded the pitch and the celebrations began. For the second time in eight years, relegation to Division III had been followed by instant promotion.

Amid the jubilation, the portents for the future were not good. Chairman Bob Grogan warned that the club was living on a knife edge with a debt of £1.5 million and was in danger of folding unless there was better support. Ashurst had performed a miracle in winning promotion for a total outlay of only £10,000, but understandably he pointed out: "I need one or two new faces...I hope I don't have to go into Division II with my hands tied".

Even before the season ended, the Bluebirds suffered a blow as Hemmerman's career came to an end in the final game, when he injured his knee ligaments against Bristol Rovers. The following season financial restraints led toDave Bennett's move to Coventry, where he scored a vital goal in Coventry's Cup Final victory against Spurs in 1987. His brother moved to Sunderland and, as little money was available for new players, it was inevitable that the side would once again struggle at a higher level.

The teams for the match between City and Leyton Orient. In the Orient side were Peter Kitchen, a former Bluebird, and Mervyn Day who played for West Ham in the 1980 Cup Final.

Teams:
Cardiff City: Dibble; Jones, Mullen, Tong, Dwyer, Bennett (G), Bennett (D), Gibbins, Hatton, Hemmerman, Lewis: Bodin (sub. not used).
Leyton Orient: Day; Roffey, Peach, Foster, Gray, Silkman, Smith (sub. Godfrey), Cornwell, Houchen, Kitchen, McNeil.

The cover of the programme for the match between Wales and Scotland in 1985. It was the second time in eight years these two nations had met at a decisive stage in the qualifying stages of the World Cup.

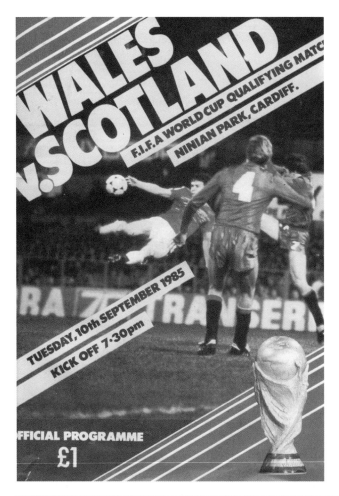

A near miss in the Welsh goalmouth as Mickey Thomas and Neville Southall manage to scramble the ball away.

MORE FALSE DAWNS

At the end of the 1984-85 season Cardiff City again dropped down to Division III. For the next 15 years the Bluebirds were the yo-yo club of the Football League, suffering relegation four more times and celebrating promotion on three occasions, a period of hope and despair interspersed with occasional cup success. There were false dawns also for a very good Welsh team which failed to qualify for any of the European or World Cup finals.

World Cup Qualifier, Tuesday 10 September 1985

Wales (1) 1 Scotland (0) 1

Victory in this match would take Wales to the finals of the World Cup for the first time since 1958. The team had already won the away match at Hampden Park and had defeated Spain, the other big name in the group. Unfortunately they had thrown away vital points against Iceland and Norway but, with players of the calibre of Neville Southall, Ian Rush, Mark Hughes and Kevin Ratcliffe, Welsh hopes of qualification were high.

The game was never a classic but the crowd of 40,000 saw plenty of incident as both sides fought a bruising battle for supremacy. After three minutes Mark Hughes launched a late tackle at Alex McLeish, who took his revenge with a ferocious tackle on Ian Rush, for which he was given a yellow card. After 12 minutes Wales took the lead with a glorious goal. Nicholas sent a low cross to **Hughes** who, from 15 yards and without checking his stride, drove a low shot past the helpless Leighton.

Dutch referee Jan Keitzer awards Scotland a controversial penalty and so once again Welsh hopes of qualifying for the finals of the World Cup are shattered.

The temperature rose on the field as the referee, Jan Keitzer, showed far too much leniency and both sides were guilty of cynical fouls. Yet Wales seemed to be well in control and had the better chances, most of which fell to Hughes. He came close with a spectacular scissors kick which just went over the bar, and just before half-time Leighton fumbled a high cross. As Hughes closed in, Leighton saved the day with a courageous dive to his feet.

The encounter left the Scottish goalkeeper dazed and he was replaced by Rough as the second half began. Eight minutes after half-time the pendulum swung towards the Scots as Jock Stein made an inspired substitution. Gordon Strachan was replaced by Davie Cooper and, as he consistently brushed aside a tiring Joey Jones, it was now a case of Wales hanging on to their slender lead. As Scotland laid siege to the Welsh goal, the men in red defended desperately.

Jock Stein collapses at the end of the World Cup match. He was one of the great managers in British football and his death put the result of the match into context.

It seemed they might hold out for a famous victory but ten minutes from the end came the moment that broke Welsh hearts. A scissors kick from David Speedie struck the hand of Dave Phillips as he instinctively tried to protect his face. To the horror of Welsh supporters Mr. Keizer pointed to the penalty spot. **Cooper** made no mistake with the kick and it was the Scots who were bound for the finals in Mexico. Eight years earlier Scotland had put Wales out of the World Cup with a similar, controversial penalty, when it was clearly a Scottish player, Joe Jordan, who had handled the ball.

Disappointed though the Welsh team were, the events on the field were put into perspective after the game. Two minutes from time Jock Stein, the popular Scottish manager, collapsed on the touchline. He had suffered a heart attack ten years earlier and had been unwell before the match. He was taken on a stretcher to the Ninian Park medical room where paramedics, ambulance-men and his personal heart specialist tried to revive him. After 25 minutes he was pronounced dead and the joy of the Scottish team and its supporters turned to tears.

Aged 62, Jock Stein was recognised as one of the most successful managers in the game. In 1967 Celtic, under his leadership, became the first British team to win the European Cup. He also had connections with South Wales as he had once played for Llanelly. Alun Evans, Secretary of the Welsh FA, paid this tribute: "He was an absolute gentleman with a lot of simple dignity and a lot of style".

The teams:

Wales: Southall; van den Hauwe, Jones; Ratcliffe, Jackett, Phillips; James, Nicholas, Rush, Hughes, Thomas.

Scotland: Leighton; Gough, Malpas; Aitken, McLeish, Miller; Nicol, Strachan (sub. Cooper), Sharp, Bett, Speedie.

Football League Division IV: Monday 2 May 1988

Cardiff City (2) 2 Crewe Alexandra (0) 0

After the Bluebirds dropped into the Fourth Division in 1986, Frank Burrows was appointed manager of Cardiff City. In his first year, the team finished just below halfway, often playing before crowds of less than 2,000 but, by the time the 1987-88 season began, Burrows had assembled a side capable of challenging for promotion. He paid Newport £22,000 for Terry Boyle, a tough tackling centre-half. In the summer of 1987 Jimmy Gilligan was signed from Lincoln for a fee of £17,500. He and Kevin Bartlett, a speedy forward who cost the Bluebirds nothing, formed a free scoring partnership that yielded more than 30 league goals in their promotion campaign. Other free transfers included Nicky Platnauer, who rarely missed a match in his three years at Cardiff, Alan Curtis, a superb midfield general, and Nigel Stephenson, his former team mate at Swansea.

The experience and skill of Alan Curtis was a major factor in taking City to promotion in 1988. Here he takes on Maurice Doyle in the match against Crewe.

By February the team had firmly established its promotion credentials though attendances were still rarely above 4,000. Against Crewe, a crowd of 10,125, easily the largest of the season, was attracted to the game in the knowledge that a point would be enough to clinch promotion.

In an entertaining first half, City gave a confident, almost arrogant display as the team played some of its best football of the season. After 13 minutes Mike Ford played a one-two with **Bartlett,** who looped the ball over the head of Dean Greygoose, the Crewe keeper, to give the Bluebirds the lead. Bartlett's pace and Brian McDermott's drive from midfield continued to trouble the Crewe defence. A McDermott corner almost led to a second goal from Ford whose effort was kicked off the line. After several near misses, it was **McDermott** who scored almost on the stroke

Dean Greygoose, the Crewe goalkeeper, flaps at Brian McDermott's corner and the ball goes straight into the net for City's second goal.

of half-time. Greygoose was unable to collect his vicious, dipping corner and, despite an attempt to clear the ball by another defender, the linesman confirmed that it had crossed the line.

A black cat raced across the pitch at half-time, suggesting that this was going to be City's day and so it proved. In some ways the second half was an anti-climax as Crewe fought back and tested the mettle of the Cardiff defence. A free kick from Stuart Ritchie was tipped over the bar by George Wood and Wakeley Gage had a goal disallowed for offside. The final whistle was the signal for a pitch invasion by the fans. After the disasters of recent years, they finally had something to celebrate. A few days later City completed a successful campaign by defeating Wrexham 2-0 at the Vetch Field to win the Welsh Cup.

It was a triumph for Frank Burrows, a down to earth character always easily recognised by the familiar flat cap. He had given the fans something to cheer about and is justly remembered as one of City's most popular managers. His promotion team was assembled at a cost of less than £40,000 but it was clear it would need strengthening in the Third Division.

Alan Curtis and Nigel Stephenson (number 5) watch as this shot from Mike Ford is blocked by Greygoose.

There was a euphoric mood after the game. The club chairman, Tony Clemo, promised that money would be made available and promotion was just a stepping stone back to respectability. Familiar words came from managing director Ron Jones: "We're on our way back to the big time and this time we plan to stay there". Instead, the following season he left for pastures new. A year later Burrows decided enough was enough and joined him at Portsmouth as assistant coach. As financial losses mounted, Clemo tried to find a buyer for the club. Bartlett, Gilligan and Ford were all sold in an attempt to balance the books. After two brief seasons in the Third Division, the club was once more relegated to the basement of the Football League.

City players show their delight as the team is promoted after two years in the Fourth Division. The team finished on a high note, winning its last eight League and Welsh Cup matches.

Teams:
Cardiff City: Wood; Bater, Platnauer, Ford, Stephenson, Boyle, Curtis, McDermott, Gilligan, Kelly, Bartlett (sub. Wheeler): Mardenborough (sub. not used).
Crewe Alexandra: Greygoose; Goodison, Edwards, Ritchie, Macowat, Wakeley, Gage, Fishenden, Harris, Cutler (sub. Eli), Doyle, Parker (sub. Morton).

Saturday 1 May 1993, Barclay's League Division III

Cardiff City (1) 2 Shrewsbury Town (1) 1

Following relegation in 1990 the Bluebirds were close to bankruptcy, struggling both on and off the field. A self-made businessman, Rick Wright, appeared to be a saviour when he offered the club enough cash to make some loan signings and cover immediate expenses. By the beginning of the 1992-93 season Wright had taken over the club and, apart from providing funds for new players, he made a number of improvements to the stadium.

Phil Stant signed for the Bluebirds in December 1992 and his 11 goals in 24 matches were a major contribution to City's success that season.

This was the first season of the new Premier League and, following the re-organisation of the rest of the Football League, the Fourth Division was now re-named Division III. Wright had appointed Eddie May as City manager and he made some shrewd signings. One of them was Phil Stant who had an impressive goal scoring record in the lower divisions of the Football League. Kevin Ratcliffe was another. His greatest days were behind him but he was still a magnificent defender. He was capped 59 times for Wales and was part of an Everton team in the 1980s that won almost every honour in the game.

After Christmas the team was almost invincible as it won 14 out of 15 matches. Promotion was achieved in mid-April with a win at Wrexham and this game with Shrewsbury attracted a crowd of 17,253, the second largest attendance in the entire Barclay's League. It seemed that optimism had returned to Ninian Park.

The game had a carnival atmosphere from the beginning as City laid siege to the Shrewsbury penalty area, but it was not until the 35th minute that the visitors' defence was breached. A curling free kick from Nathan Blake was met by **Jason Perry** who bravely dived through a crowd of players to head an excellent goal. Celebrations were cut short as **Kevin Summerfield**, a former City player, profiting from a mix-up between Gavin Ward and Ratcliffe, equalised with a shot from just inside the penalty area.

At half-time Chris Pike replaced Carl Dale, and he almost scored immediately when his shot from a narrow angle was saved by Edwards. City's winner came after 55 minutes, when **Blake** met a cross from Brazil to slide the ball into the net for his 14th goal of the season. Both sides were playing attractive football and, as Shrewsbury pressed for a second equaliser, Ward made some uncharacteristic mistakes to give his defence a few anxious moments. Kevin Ratcliffe was clearly suffering from an injury and ten minutes from the end he left the field to a standing ovation.

With two minutes remaining, some "comedian" in the crowd blew a whistle and the spectators, thinking the game was over, spilled on to the field. Police horses occupied the centre of the pitch and a warning that the game might be abandoned, was enough to restore order. In all five minutes of extra time were added before the celebrations could officially begin.

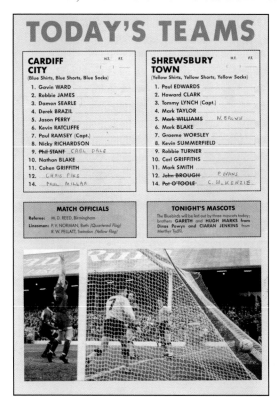

The team sheet for the game with Shrewsbury showed a number of changes for both teams. Stant had to miss this game because of an injury and his place was taken by Carl Dale.

Jason Perry was not a frequent goal scorer but this spectacular, flying header gave City the lead against Shrewsbury.

The following Saturday, 5,000 cheering City fans made the journey to Scunthorpe to see the Bluebirds win 3-0, thus clinching the Third Division Championship. On 16 May, at the National Stadium, Cardiff completed a very successful season by beating Rhyl 5-0 to win the Welsh Cup. The completion of the double allowed Rick Wright to recoup much of his investment in Cardiff City through an insurance policy which now paid him £1.4 million.

Hopes were high that promotion would be a stepping stone to better days. The problem was that Rick Wright was never really interested in football, nor did he hide his feelings. He always made it clear that, after two years at the helm, he expected someone else to take up the burden of running Cardiff City. No-one rushed to accept the challenge and a few months later Wright withdrew his financial support for the club.

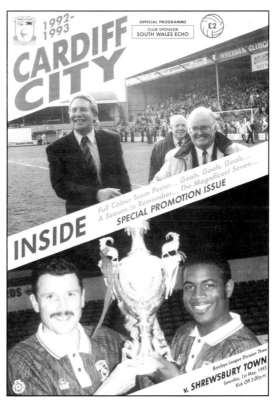

In this special programme Eddie May (left) and Rick Wright celebrate the promotion won at Wrexham a week earlier. Below Paul Ramsey (left) and Nathan Blake proudly show off the Welsh Cup that City had won the previous season.

Saturday 29 January 1994: FA Cup Round Four

Cardiff City (0) 1 Manchester City (0) 0

The 1993-94 season once more saw Cardiff City struggling to avoid relegation as key players left the club. The only consolation for supporters was a cup run in which the team excelled itself. In the third round the Bluebirds had collected a notable scalp as they defeated Middlesbrough from Division I after a replay. The reward was an attractive home tie against Manchester City, a side languishing in the lower reaches of the Premier Division, but firm favourites to win against their lower League opponents. Before the match the *Western Mail* speculated that the game would provide a "shop window" for Nathan Blake, City's star player and the latest to be a target for other clubs. The crowd of 20,486 was the largest for many years, even though the match was being shown "live" on BBC Wales TV.

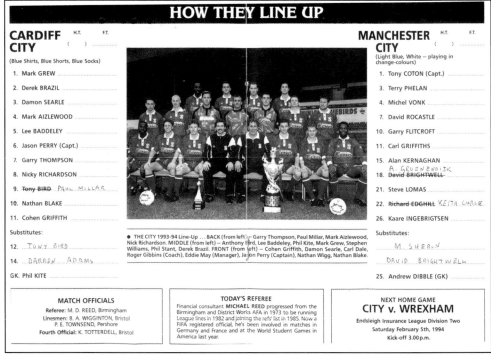

Paul Millar replaced Tony Bird in the starting line-up against Manchester City. For the visitors, Keith Curle and Groenendijk played instead of David Brightwell and Richard Edghill.

Blake and Garry Thompson soon caused problems among the visitors' defence as the Bluebirds refused to be overawed by their Premiership opponents. After ten minutes Thompson fired in a shot from 20 yards which brought a fine save from Tony Coton, widely regarded as one of the best goalkeepers in England. Cardiff continued to create the better chances but half-time arrived without any goals.

In the second period City continued to match their visitors, though Manchester might have taken the lead after 50 minutes when Gary Flitcroft's shot was kicked off the line by Damon Searle. Eventually the outcome of the match hinged on two incidents. The first came in the 64th minute when **Blake** put Cardiff ahead with a magnificent solo goal. Collecting a throw-in from Cohen Griffith with his back towards the Manchester goal, he then pivoted and waltzed past three defenders, before chipping the ball into the net past a helpless Coton.

Ten minutes from the end came the second crucial moment of the afternoon. A poor clearance from Mark Grew was picked up by David Rocastle who was brought down by Searle inside the penalty area. Spectators held their breath as Keith Curle hit the ball to Grew's left but the City goalkeeper made up for his earlier blunder by holding on to the

Nathan Blake's superb individual goal takes the Bluebirds into the fifth round of the Cup. Keith Curle vainly attempts to intercept.

ball at the second attempt. It was the seventh time out of ten that he had saved a penalty. The City were through to the fifth round and Brian Horton, the Manchester City manager, admitted, "We were outplayed...they deserved it". Stan Hey of *The Independent*, commented, "Cardiff's second half performance would have been sufficient to threaten even Manchester's other team".

Grew's heroics might have been enough to make him man of the match had it not been for the brilliance of Nathan Blake. His ball control and ability to score spectacular goals had been a key factor in the promotion campaign a year earlier.

City's Garry Thompson, who was standing in for the injured Phil Stant, sends Manchester City skipper, Keith Curle, the wrong way.

Unfortunately the goal that won this match proved to be his last for the City. He was locked in a pay dispute with the club and Rick Wright was unwilling to offer him improved terms. The Bluebirds' reward for their giant killing act was another home tie against Luton but, by the time it was played, Blake had been transferred to Sheffield United for £300,000. Without his magic, City's FA Cup run came to an end as Luton won the match comfortably 2-1.

The cover of the match programme for the cup-tie with Manchester City. The photograph shows Nathan Blake's winner against Middlesborough in the third round.

Wright's attempts to sell the club finally met with success as Samesh Kumar, a former chairman of Birmingham City, took up the reins. Money continued to be tight as the club entered upon its worst period since the 1930s. In 1995 the Bluebirds were again relegated and a year later the club finished third from bottom in the Third Division. Matters improved in 1997 when Cardiff reached the play-offs but a year later the team was once more languishing near the bottom of Division III. Heavily in debt and with one of the worst sides in the Football League, the future appeared bleak.

Nationwide League Division III: Saturday 30 January 1999

Cardiff City (2) 4 Brentford (0) 1

In an effort to revive the fortunes of the club, the directors invited Frank Burrows to return to Cardiff and, once again with little money available, he forged a side capable of winning promotion. His greatest acquisition was full-back Mark Delaney who was signed from Carmarthen Town. He soon became a firm favourite at Ninian Park, not just for his defensive skills but also for his surging runs down the right wing. His stay at Cardiff lasted less than a year, and in March 1999 he was sold to Aston Villa for £500,000. Other inspired signings included the ex- Swansea duo, Andy Legg and Jason Bowen, and Mike Ford who returned from Oxford to captain the team. Leading the attack were Kevin Nugent, who joined Cardiff from Bristol City in 1997, and John Williams, another of Burrows' free transfer bargains.

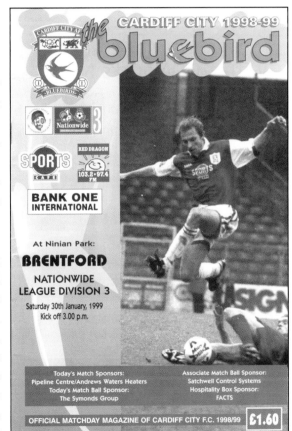

The Bluebirds were top of the table when Brentford came to Ninian Park. A few weeks earlier the Bees had beaten the City 1-0 at Griffin Park and were themselves promotion contenders. One of the best crowds of the season, 11,509, saw Cardiff win an excellent game with a display of football far above Third Division standard.

From the outset, the Bluebirds' first time tackling and harrying took the sting out of the Brentford attack. Jon Hallworth had only one save to make in the first half and, once the midfield battle was won, Brentford had no answer to the pace of John Williams and the guile of Nugent. After 20 minutes Herman Hreidarsson, an Icelandic international who cost Brentford

Richard Carpenter, seen here on the cover of the programme for the Brentford match, was one of Frank Burrows' more expensive signings. He cost £35,000 when he joined the City from Fulham in the summer of 1998.

£750,000, was hustled off the ball by Delaney and from his centre **Williams** headed his 15th goal of the season. Another soaring header from **Jeff Eckhardt,** following good approach work by Carpenter and Jason Fowler, put Cardiff 2-0 ahead in the 28th minute.

The goal of the match came seven minutes into the second half. Jason Fowler received the ball from Nugent after Craig Middleton had won a challenge in midfield.

Andy Legg battles for a high ball with a Brentford defender, while Mark Delaney and another Brentford player wait to see the outcome

As Woodman advanced to meet him, **Fowler** chipped the ball over the goalkeeper's head with pinpoint accuracy. Fowler had a talent for scoring spectacular goals and this was one which would have graced any occasion. Brentford pulled a goal back when **Danny Boxall** hit a powerful shot from just outside the penalty area, but 15 minutes from the end the Bluebirds restored their three goal advantage. Woodman fumbled a shot from Williams and, as the Brentford defence panicked, **Nugent** was on hand to take advantage. Characteristically Burrows described it as, "a bit of a scruff-bag goal" but quickly added, "All Cardiff City goals look good to me".

The Bluebirds remained three points ahead at the top of the table and, though they fell away a little towards the end of the season, achieved automatic promotion in third place. Ironically it was Brentford who went up as champions.

Jason Fowler was a player who lacked consistency but had considerable skill. In this photograph he shows his ability as he surges forward, leaving three Brentford defenders trailing in his wake.

The result against Brentford was a well-timed present for Frank Burrows on his 55th birthday. It was also Cardiff's eighth successive home win in the league.

The side appeared to have enough ability to hold its own in what was now called Division II, especially as the signing of Willie Boland from Coventry added strength to the squad. Prophetically the *South Wales Echo*, reviewing the ups and downs of recent years, warned: "The roller coaster could take another of those terrible twists and turns at any time". So it proved. The following January, Frank Burrows left once again to become assistant coach at West Bromwich. In May 2000, after a single season in Division II, Bluebird fans once more suffered the disappointment of promotion followed by speedy relegation. For the fourth time in 15 years, City were back in the bottom tier of the League.

Teams:
Cardiff City: Hallworth; Delaney, Ford (sub. Legg) Mitchell, Eckhardt, Carpenter, Fowler, O'Sullivan, Williams, Nugent, Middleton: Bowen (sub. not used)
Brentford: Woodman; Boxall, Anderson, Hreidarsson, Quinn, Bates, Freeman, Aspinall, Mahon, Rowlands (sub. Oatway), Scott (sub. Owusu).

THE END OF AN ERA

Steve Borley, a lifelong Bluebirds' supporter, took over as chairman from Samesh Kumar in 1999 but, after another disappointing season, it was clear that substantial investment was needed if the club was to make the progress its supporters expected. A year later Sam Hammam, the former owner of Wimbledon, took over the club. His arrival aroused hopes that at last the sleeping giant could awaken from his slumbers. Hammam was a dynamic figure who put forward radical plans for the club's future, including the building of a new stadium to replace Ninian Park. New players were brought in and in three seasons the Bluebirds were twice promoted. City fans were grateful to Hammam for bringing them long overdue success, but unfortunately it was done at the expense of financial prudence. By 2004 a huge debt threatened to force the club into liquidation.

A year later Sam Hammam invited Peter Ridsdale, who had been through a similar situation at Leeds, to join the club. Hammam resigned in October 2006 and new investors with Ridsdale as chairman took over the club. The debt was renegotiated and the green light was given to begin work on the new stadium. It is now close to completion and excellent training facilities have been found in the Vale of Glamorgan. On the playing side Dave Jones, with little money to spend, has produced a team that is holding its own in the Championship. Repayment of its debt continued to be a cloud hanging over the club but in 2008 the team achieved what most people thought was the impossible dream, when Cardiff City appeared in the Cup Final at Wembley.

FA Cup Round Three: Sunday 6 January 2002

Cardiff City (1) 2 Leeds United (1) 1

In 2001 Cardiff finally escaped from the Third Division and this time the team was capable of competing at a higher level. To add to the excitement of what was already a promising season, the Bluebirds were drawn to play Leeds United in the FA Cup. Few gave Cardiff much chance as United were leading the Premiership and were still involved in the UEFA Cup. Among the team's host of internationals were such star names as Robbie Fowler, Mark Viduka, Rio Ferdinand, Alan Smith, Danny Mills and Jonathan Woodgate. Though the game was being televised by Sky Sport, a capacity crowd of 22,000 welcomed the teams as they were led on to the field by the great John Charles, who had played for both clubs.

Leeds suffered a blow after a few minutes as Ferdinand was injured in a collision with Gavin Gordon and was substituted by Michael Duberry. Otherwise, the early stages of the match went according to the script. After 12 minutes Spencer Prior hit a wayward clearance straight to Gary Kelly who passed to **Viduka**. The Australian made no mistake with a shot from 20 yards that gave Alexander no chance. There may have been fears that City were about to be humiliated but, after that opening goal, the game turned into an even contest. The crowd, already voluble, raised the volume another

THE CHARLES LINK

BIG JOHN – A LEEDS UNITED, CARDIFF CITY AND WALES LEGEND

John takes out Leeds for the last time (above left) before his summer 1957 transfer to Juventus.
(Above right) August 1963, and he makes his first Cardiff City appearance in our pre-season public practice game.
(Below) in action for Wales at Ninian Park during October 1956 as he gets in a shot, challenged by
Scotland's George Young. In the background is the old covered Grange End.

This tribute to John Charles appeared in the programme for the game with Leeds in 2002. John came to Cardiff late in his career but still fulfilled a major role for the club, inspiring the younger players around him.

decibel as the Bluebirds harried their illustrious opponents. Prior, despite his early mistake, Gabbidon, and Scott Young all gave the Leeds forwards few opportunities. Graham Kavanagh and Legg were inspirational in midfield and the speed of Rob Earnshaw was giving Harte a torrid time.

The City equaliser came within nine minutes. After Alan Smith had fouled Andy Legg 25 yards from goal, **Kavanagh** hit a curling, swerving shot past the helpless

Danny Gabbidon was a magnificent defender for Cardiff City. Here he dispossesses Mark Viduka in the match with Leeds.

Referee Andy D'Urso had little option but to show Alan Smith a red card in a fiery cup-tie because of this foul on Andy Legg that left him with blood pouring from his mouth.

Martyn. Later he claimed he had been practising free kicks like this all through the week. Both sides had chances to score but the next key moment in this breathtaking cup-tie came just before half-time. Andy Legg pulled Smith back and the Leeds player lashed out with his arm, striking Legg in the mouth. The City player was booked for his part in the affray but referee D'Urso had no hesitation in showing Smith a red card. Leeds players furiously accused Legg of cheating but there was no doubt that the referee had made the correct decision. That did not stop the Leeds manager, David O'Leary, from claiming it was another example of referees victimising Smith.

In the second half, Cardiff were able to do most of the attacking with the advantage of an extra man but Leeds always posed a threat, especially as the Bluebirds began to tire. In the 75th minute Viduka broke through the City defence but, as he was about to shoot, Young made the greatest tackle of his life as he came from behind to knock the ball away.

Leeds seemed to be settling for a replay at Elland Road but in the closing minutes the City forced four corners in quick succession. From the last of these Leo Fortune-West, who had replaced Gavin Gordon a few minutes earlier, headed down a Kavanagh corner. The ball bounced off Harte's shin, and from eight yards **Scott Young** slammed the ball past Martyn to send the crowd wild with excitement. It was

Scott Young smashes the ball into the net against Leeds and the Bluebirds have won a famous victory.

too late for Leeds to make a come-back, and three minutes later City had created the surprise result of the round. Understandably Scott was chosen as the man of the match.

It was now that events off the field triggered controversy. Many jubilant City fans invaded the pitch and some of them confronted the Leeds supporters. Objects, such as coins and plastic bottles, were thrown and newspaper headlines of "War Zone" and "Mayhem" took much of the gloss away from a magnificent Cardiff achievement. Though there were ugly scenes, South Wales Police confirmed that most City fans were, "well behaved if understandably exuberant". In fact there were just four arrests and the worst casualty

The cover of the programme for the cup-tie between Cardiff and Leeds. The match was marked by controversy on and off the field but it proved to be one of the great days in Cardiff City's history

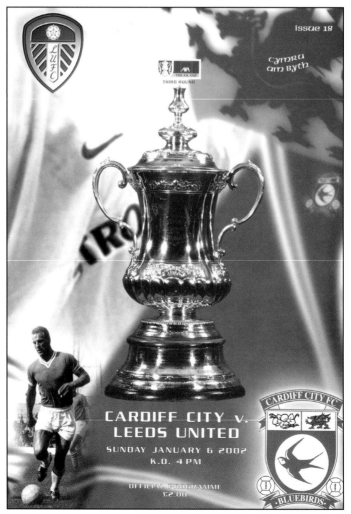

was probably a Leeds supporter who was bitten by a police dog as he boarded a bus. Unfortunately the bad behaviour by a small minority made the headlines and tarnished the reputation of the club.

Since that day little has gone right for Leeds United. Players had to be sold and that glittering array of internationals was broken up. The lowest point came in May 2007 when the club was relegated to what used to be the third tier of the Football League. For Cardiff, the fourth round of the Cup proved to be an anti- climax as the Bluebirds were defeated 3-1 at Tranmere. FA Cup sponsors, AXA, later named the City as "Giantkillers" of the season and scenes off the field could not take away the joy of a wonderful achievement.

Teams:
Cardiff City: Alexander; Gabbidon, Prior, Young, Legg; Boland, Bonner, Kavanagh, Brayson; Earnshaw, Gordon (sub. Fortune-West).
Leeds United: Martyn; Mills, Woodgate, Ferdinand (sub. Duberry), Harte, Kelly, Bowyer, Batty, Smith; Viduka, Fowler.

Nationwide League Division II
Play-off Semi-final Second Leg:
Wednesday 1 May 2002

Cardiff City (0) 0 Stoke City (0) 2 (after extra time)

In an attempt to build a team capable of challenging for Division I of the Nationwide League, Sam Hammam spent £7 million on new players. Peter Thorne and Graham Kavanagh both came from Stoke and cost over £1 million each. Defenders Danny Gabbidon and Spencer Prior were only slightly less expensive and substantial sums were paid for Neil Alexander, the young Scottish goalkeeper, and Leo Fortune-West, who scored some important goals in the two seasons he spent with the club.

Despite this spending spree, Cardiff's promotion challenge was faltering in February and, following a 4-0 defeat at Wigan, Lennie Lawrence replaced Alan Cork as manager. What followed was an astonishing, unbeaten run as the team won ten and drew three of their remaining fixtures. These results included a record 7-1 away win at Oldham where Andy Campbell, recently bought from Middlesborough for £900,000, scored a hat-trick.

The Bluebirds had good reason to be confident as they prepared for a semi-final play-off with Stoke. In the first leg of the tie everything went according to plan. Leo Fortune-West and Robert Earnshaw, now fulfilling his potential as an exciting goal scorer, gave City a two goal lead. Late in the game, Deon Burton reduced the arrears for Stoke but, with the home leg to come, a 2-1 victory was a satisfactory result. Despite that defeat, Stoke still felt confident, regarding Burton's goal as a lifeline. It was also their third consecutive play-off semi-final and that experience was to show in the second leg of the tie.

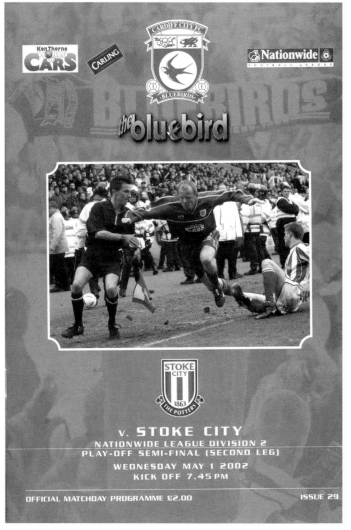

The programme cover for the second leg of the play-off semi-final against Stoke. In his notes Lennie Lawrence wrote that the first goal in this game would be vital. How right he was!

From the beginning Stoke defended as though their lives depended on it, while the City players seemed to be suffering from nerves. Kavanagh, so often an inspiration in midfield, fell below his usual standards and Earnshaw was being caught offside far too often. Tension grew as Stoke dominated the midfield and created the better chances. Burton shot wide after beating the offside trap and just before half-time Iwelumo skied the ball over the bar from close range.

Stoke continued to look the more likely team to score in the second half and only occasionally did City's attack appear dangerous. The best opportunity fell to Thorne, who met an overhead kick from Earnshaw with a flying header that Cutler just managed to grab on the line. Despite their sub-standard performance, it seemed the Bluebirds were going to hold on for the goal-less draw that would take them to a play-off final at the Millennium Stadium. In the very last minute came the cruel twist of fate that ruined City's season,

Leo Fortune-West won this heading duel despite the close attention of two Stoke defenders in the play-off semi-final.

as Gudjonsson hit a cross from Clarke into the path of **O'Connor**, who hooked the ball into the corner of the net.

The aggregate score was level and City supporters were stunned as the game went into extra time. With five minutes remaining, the prospect of a penalty shoot-out was looming, when the referee gave Stoke a dubious free kick on the edge of the Cardiff penalty area for an alleged foul by Prior. **O'Connor's** drive took a wicked deflection that gave Alexander no chance. Prior was sent off for calling the referee a cheat and, to make

Robert Earnshaw found it difficult to break away from the close marking of a Stoke defender who appears to be handling the ball.

HOW WE FINISHED 2001/02
NATIONWIDE LEAGUE DIV. 2

TEAMS	P	HOME W	D	L	F	A	AWAY W	D	L	F	A (GD)	Pts.
1. Brighton & H. A	46	17	5	1	42–16		8	10	5	24–26(+24)		90
2. Reading	46	12	7	4	36–20		11	8	4	34–23(+27)		84
3. Brentford	46	17	5	1	48–12		7	6	10	29–31(+34)		83
4. CARDIFF CITY	46	12	8	3	39–25		11	6	6	36–25(+25)		83
5. Stoke City	46	16	4	3	43–12		7	7	9	24–28(+27)		80
6. Huddersfield T	46	13	7	3	35–19		8	8	7	30–28(+18)		78
7. Bristol City	46	13	6	4	38–21		8	4	11	30–32(+15)		73
8. Q.P.R	46	11	10	2	35–18		8	4	11	25–31(+11)		71
9. Oldham Athletic	46	14	6	3	47–27		4	10	9	30–38(+12)		70
10. Wigan Athletic	46	9	6	8	36–23		7	10	6	30–28(+15)		64
11. Wycombe W.	46	13	5	5	38–26		4	8	11	20–38 (-6)		64
12. Tranmere R.	46	10	9	4	39–19		6	6	11	24–41 (+3)		63
13. Swindon Town	46	10	7	6	26–21		5	7	11	20–35 (-10)		59
14. Port Vale	46	11	6	6	35–24		5	4	14	16–38 (-11)		58
15. Colchester Utd.	46	9	6	8	35–33		6	6	11	30–43 (-11)		57
16. Blackpool	46	8	9	6	39–31		6	5	12	27–38 (-3)		56
17. Peterborough	46	11	5	7	46–26		4	5	14	18–33 (+5)		55
18. Chesterfield	46	9	3	11	35–36		4	10	9	18–29 (-12)		52
19. Notts County.	46	8	7	8	28–29		5	4	14	31–42 (-12)		50
20. Northampton T	46	9	4	10	30–33		5	3	15	24–46 (-25)		49
21. AFC Bournemouth	46	9	4	10	36–33		1	10	12	20–38 (-15)		44
22. Bury	46	6	9	8	26–32		5	2	16	17–43 (-32)		44
23. Wrexham	46	7	7	9	29–32		4	3	16	27–57 (-33)		43
24. Cambridge Utd.	46	7	7	9	29–34		0	6	17	18–59 (-46)		34

matters worse, there were scenes of hooliganism afterwards that once more tainted the good name of City supporters. It was Stoke who won the play-off final ten days later and Cardiff who would spend another season in Division II. As Lennie Lawrence said, "It's the nature of the play-offs, that if you put in one below par performance, that's it".

The final table for the 2001-2 season shows how close the Bluebirds were to the automatic promotion that would have avoided the agony of that play-off with Stoke.

Teams:

Cardiff City: Alexander; Weston, Young, Prior, Croft, Boland, Kavanagh, Bonner (sub. Maxwell), Fortune-West, Earnshaw (sub. Campbell), Thorne (sub. Bowen); Bywater, Collins, (subs not used).

Stoke City: Cutler; Thomas, Handyside, Shtanluk, Clarke, Gudjonsson, O'Connor, Dinning (sub. Vandeurzen), Gunnlaugsson (sub. Cooke), Iwelumo (sub. Oulare), Burton; Viander, Brightwell, (subs. not used)

Nationwide League Division II
Play-off Semi-final First Leg:
Saturday 10 May 2003

Cardiff City 1 (0) Bristol City (0) 0

A year later Cardiff City players and supporters again faced the nerve racking experience of the play-offs. This time there was little of the optimism from a year earlier. Hopes of gaining automatic promotion were not realised, though Earnshaw had an outstanding season in scoring 31 League goals to create a new club record.

Cardiff City faced the play-offs again a year later. This time there was apprehension rather than optimism as they faced their bogy side, Bristol City.

Finishing sixth in the League was just enough to scrape into the play-offs but a semi-final against Bristol City appeared a daunting task. It was 11 years since Cardiff had beaten their rivals from across the Severn. The Robins were Cardiff's bogy side and had won both League matches during the season.

Bearing in mind the disappointment of a year earlier, and recognising that Bristol were the firm favourites, the Supporters' Club contributor wrote a light-hearted comment in the match programme: "The Bluebirds can relax and just enjoy the experience of the play-offs…sing our hearts out for the boys and you never know, we may be singing all the way to Division One – oops! We're getting carried away".

A crowd of 19,000, the largest of the season, came prepared for what Lennie Lawrence had called an "ultra competitive match" and so it proved. It was never a classic and defences were usually on top. Neither goalkeeper was troubled very often, though Neil Alexander made a vital save from a Christian Roberts' header that appeared goal-bound after eight minutes.

Andy Legg began his career with Swansea and came to Cardiff in the twilight of his career. His total commitment to the Bluebirds was never more apparent than in the play-off matches of 2003.

Gabbidon and Prior were outstanding at the heart of the Cardiff defence, while Chris Barker ensured that Scott Murray, Bristol's most dangerous forward, had few opportunities. Andy Legg, who had endeared himself to the Ninian Park faithful for his tireless displays over the last five years, covered every blade of grass until his substitution by Mark Bonner late in the game.

It was difficult to see either side scoring when, in the 75th minute, Tommy Doherty, one of Bristol's most impressive players, slipped and lost the ball to Peter Thorne. He passed to Willie Boland on the right and the Irishman provided a perfect centre for **Thorne** to head Cardiff into the lead. Earnshaw might have

Peter Thorne, who scored the winning goal in the first leg of the semi-final,, battles it out with a Bristol City defender.

scored a second, when he burst through with only Phillips to beat but the Bristol keeper kept the tie alive with a brilliant save.

It was one of Cardiff's best displays of the season but the job was only half done. The Robins were confident they could overturn City's lead at Ashton Gate, where they had an excellent home record and had scored 43 League goals that season. The pressure on the Bluebirds was still intense but they were better equipped to deal with it than a year earlier. The players were under no illusions that a tough second leg awaited them but there was a steely determination to make up for their disappointment 12 months ago.

The return match was certainly not for the faint-hearted. It was inevitable that

Spencer Prior (right) and Lee Peacock both go for a high ball in the play-off with Bristol City.

Andy Campbell races past QPR defender, Danny Shittu, to score the winner at the Millennium Stadium and take the Bluebirds into Division I.

Bristol would do most of the attacking but once again the City defence was magnificent. The most heart-stopping moment came near the end, when a diving header from Tinnion seemed destined for the back of the net. Somehow, to the disbelief of Bristol supporters and the joy of the City fans, Alexander managed to push the ball around the post.

The match finished 0-0 and City were through to a play-off final at the Millennium Stadium against Queens Park Rangers. Again strong nerves were a necessity as the game went into extra time. With a penalty shoot-out imminent, Andy Campbell sent the City fans into seventh heaven with the only goal of the game. Little went right for Andy afterwards but he will always be remembered for that one glorious moment, when he scored to take Cardiff back to the old Second Division after an absence of 18 years.

Teams:
Cardiff City: Alexander; Weston, Gabbidon, Prior, Barker, Boland, Kavanagh, Legg (sub. Bonner), Whalley, Thorne, Earnshaw (sub. Campbell)
Bristol City: Phillips; Carey, Bell, Doherty (sub. Tinnion), Butler, Hill, Murray, Burnell, Peacock, Roberts (sub. Rosenior), Coles.

Coca-Cola Championship; Saturday 26 August 2006

Cardiff City (1) 2 Birmingham City (0) 0

Sam Hammam was at the height of his popularity after that success at the Millennium Stadium. The Bluebirds' first season in Division I was reasonably successful but in the following year the team narrowly avoided relegation. To make matters worse, extravagant spending had taken the club close to financial ruin and plans for the new stadium remained on hold. Earnshaw, Kavanagh, Gabbidon and one of City's rising stars, James Collins, were all sold in an attempt to balance the books. Before the start of the 2005-6 season Dave Jones was appointed as City's new manager. It proved to be the best decision the club had taken for a long time. With a reputation for building teams and with very little money available, he made use of loan signings, free transfers, and shrewd dealing in the transfer market, to shape a team capable of holding its own in the Championship.

The first fruits of this policy were shown in his second season in charge. The match against Birmingham attracted a sell-out crowd of 20,109 and was the largest for a League match since the game with Swansea in 1980. In their early games the Bluebirds had already taken ten points from four matches in impressive style. Kevin McNaughton, Glenn Loovens, Stephen McPhail and Roger Johnson were all proving themselves to be excellent signings. Perhaps the pick of Jones's acquisitions was Michael Chopra, purchased from Newcastle for £500,000. With his pace and eye for goal scoring opportunities, he was showing himself to be one of the finest strikers in the Championship. Cameron Jerome, sold to

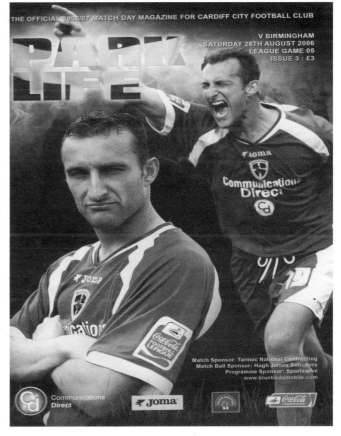

The cover of the programme for the game with Birmingham City. The crowd of more than 20,000 enjoyed one of the best matches seen at Ninian Park for many years.

Michael Chopra, one of Dave Jones's bargain buys, shows a turn of speed and ball control as he races for goal

Cardiff goalkeeper Neil Alexander seems to be in trouble and Roger Johnson (right) looks concerned as Cameron Jerome closes in, but this Birmingham attack was successfully cleared.

Birmingham for £4 million was returning to Ninian Park, though he began the game as a substitute.

From the start Cardiff outplayed Birmingham. After12 minutes Paul Parry fed a short corner to Chopra who dribbled along the by-line before passing to **Joe Ledley**. The youngster, showing great maturity, hit a left footed shot into the net. City could have added to that lead before half-time as Parry and Chopra both had good chances. Birmingham too might have scored as Alexander made a superb one-handed save to keep out a header from McSheffrey.

After the interval Cardiff continued to dominate play but Cameron Jerome, who had come off the bench to replace Campbell, had Birmingham's best opportunity. With only Alexander to beat he shot wide to shouts of, "What a waste of money" from some Cardiff supporters. He had annoyed them before his transfer with unwise

The City players are jubilant as Paul Parry scores against Birmingham to give the Bluebirds a 2-0 lead.

comments about wanting to join a bigger club. The result was put beyond doubt 15 minutes from time, when Steve Thompson beat two defenders before chipping the ball towards the far post. **Parry** was on hand to drive the ball home.

The win took the Bluebirds to the top of the Championship. It was their best ever start to a season and the quality of their football at this stage was brilliant. Their impressive form continued for several weeks and it seemed possible for Cardiff to mount a serious promotion challenge. Dave Jones was delighted with the win but was only too aware that, "Football will kick you in the teeth the moment you get carried away". Steve Bruce, the Birmingham manager, was gracious in defeat but warned that the small Cardiff squad might face difficulties, when injuries and suspensions led to the loss of key players.

So it proved. From November to January a run of disastrous results pushed the Bluebirds down to mid-table. A rally in February raised hopes of at least making the play-offs but, after failing to win any of their last nine games, City had to be content with a finish in 13th place. The game against Birmingham was an indication of the heights the team could reach but the disappointment, after such a splendid start to the season, showed that the team still needed strengthening.

Teams:
Cardiff City: Alexander; Gilbert, Loovens, Johnson, McNaughton, Ledley, Scimeca, McPhail, Thompson (sub.K. Campbell), Chopra; Flood, Glombard, Kamara, Gunter (subs. not used).
Birmingham City: Doyle; Kelly (sub. Larsson), Sadler, N'Gotty, Jaidi, Johnson, Bendtner, Natti, Dunn, McSheffrey, Campbell (sub. Jerome); Legzoins, Forssell, Tebily (subs. not used)

FA Cup Round Five: 16 February 2008

Cardiff City (2) 2 Wolverhampton Wanderers (0) 0

Cardiff City's penultimate season at Ninian Park turned out to be the most eventful in its history. Before the campaign began Michael Chopra was sold to Sunderland for £5 million, but fans found some consolation when Robbie Fowler and Jimmy Floyd Hasselbaink signed for the club. Much was expected from these veterans but unfortunately Fowler missed most of the campaign through injury.

Across the road from Ninian Park, the new stadium was taking shape but the financial problems surrounding the club stubbornly continued. It was a bombshell when Langston, the mysterious bankers who held the club's debt after Sam Hammam's resignation, demanded immediate repayment of £24 million before the season began. If upheld in court, City would have been forced into administration. The club was adamant that the debt did not have to be paid in full before 2016. The threat from Langston has not been removed completely but a court judgement in Cardiff's favour suggests a compromise will be reached.

The programme cover for the match with Wolves featured Aaron Ramsey, a talented teenager whose future now lies with Arsenal.

Poor home form gave the Bluebirds a bad start to their League programme and until December relegation appeared a possibility. Then the team at last found its true form, and a few weeks later it was mounting a promotion charge that almost took Cardiff to the play-offs. Such was the topsy-turvy nature of the Championship this season. City's challenge eventually petered out, because a shortage of cash due to the court case prevented Dave Jones from strengthening his team. The compensation for supporters lay in the excitement created by an extraordinary FA Cup run.

When the Bluebirds were drawn against non-leaguers Chasetown in the third round, no-one could have foreseen what was to follow. Five divisions separated the teams but, when Chasetown scored first, a huge cup shock appeared possible. Before half-time City rallied and won comfortably 3-1. Another away game followed at Hereford and again a professional approach ensured a 2-1 victory.

In the fifth round, the Bluebirds were rewarded with a home tie against Wolverhampton Wanderers, a team from their own division. The attendance was a disappointing 15,339 but those who stayed away missed a magnificent City performance. Since 1927 the City had never progressed beyond the fifth round of this famous competition. This was the day the Bluebirds smashed that 80 year old bogy with a display of scintillating football.

The game virtually ended as a contest after 11 minutes. Within 90 seconds a defence splitting pass from Hasselbaink sent **Whittingham** clear and, with only the Welsh international goalkeeper, Wayne Hennessey, in his path he made no mistake. Soon afterwards it was 2-0 with a superb goal from **Hasselbaink**, following good work by Parry and Whittingham.

Peter Whittingham turns away in triumph as he scores City's first goal against Wolves. Welsh international goalkeeper, Wayne Hennessey, understandably looks dejected.

Wolves never looked like recovering against a rock-solid City defence in which Glenn Loovens and Roger Johnson were outstanding. Only Freddy Eastwood, when he came on as a substitute, posed a threat and Peter Enckelman had few saves to make. In midfield Aaron Ramsey, just 17 years old, showed why he was regarded as such a great prospect. Apart from his skill he displayed a maturity far beyond his years. The pace of Paul Parry was a constant threat to the Wolves' defenders and he could have added to Cardiff's tally, while Hasselbaink crowned his finest display of the season with that magnificent goal. Wolves played poorly and their manager, Mick McCarthy, admitted, "We were hopeless and never really scratched the surface". While there was some truth in this statement, a better team than Wolves would have succumbed to a City team in this mood.

The Bluebirds were now faltering in the League but this result strengthened the belief that it could be their year in the Cup. The sixth round again brought the best out of the team with another excellent victory at

Jimmy Floyd Hasselbaink unleashes a thunderbolt for Cardiff's second goal after fooling the Wolves' defenders with a brilliant dummy.

Glenn Loovens was a tower of strength in the City defence. Here he is watched by Tony Capaldi as he rises to deal with a potential threat from the Wolves' forwards.

Middlesbrough. The Premiership team were outplayed as goals by Whittingham and Johnson took City to Wembley and a semi-final against Barnsley. Undeniably the giant killers of the season, Barnsley had beaten Liverpool and Chelsea to reach the semi-final. With Manchester United and Arsenal also out of the cup, it was now the most open competition for many years. Joe Ledley's early goal was enough to overcome the plucky Yorkshiremen and, for the first time in 81 years, the Bluebirds were in the FA Cup Final.

Three cup-ties later and, though the City lost the Cup Final, City fans at Wembley show how proud they are of their team's remarkable achievement.

For City supporters it was hard to believe and, in the six weeks leading up to the great day, the club and its fans enjoyed their unexpected fame. The final against Portsmouth proved to be "a bridge too far" and an unfortunate error by Enckelman was enough to give Pompey a narrow victory. Nevertheless, 500 million people across the world saw City match their Premiership opponents for long periods of the game. Equally importantly, the team and its supporters were applauded for their part in restoring the romance of the FA Cup which, in recent years, had seen a sad decline. The great adventure was over but what a season it had been.

Teams:
Cardiff City: Enckelman; McNaughton, Johnson, Loovens, Capaldi, Whittingham (sub. Sinclair), Rae, McPhail (sub. Blake), Ramsey, Parry, Hasselbaink (sub. Thompson); Oakes, Purse, (subs. not used).
Wolverhampton Wanderers: Hennessey; Foley (sub. Gibson), Breen, Craddock, Gray, Potter, Henry, Olofinjana (sub. Eastwood), Bothroyd, Keogh, Kyle (sub. Elliott); Slack, Edwards (subs. not used).

Ninian Park in 2008 is nearly a century old and full of nostalgic memories for City supporters, but sadly outdated in the modern era of football.

LOOKING TO THE FUTURE

Cardiff City are now entering their final season at Ninian Park and, as these pages have shown, the old ground has seen some glorious occasions for the Bluebirds and the Welsh team. There have also been moments of despair from which it seemed the club might not recover.

Until the 1960s Ninian Park was a ground comparable with most in the Football League but, for the last 40 years, its deficiencies have become ever more obvious. Other clubs have either improved existing facilities or moved into new stadiums. Nearly 50,000 spectators watched the cup-tie with Leeds United in February 1972 but it was the last time the ground would house a crowd of this magnitude. In 1977 the Safety of Sports Grounds Act led to many parts of the ground being declared unsafe. The Grangetown Stand was demolished and was replaced by a smaller uncovered terrace. A new roof was not added until 2001 and for a time the ground capacity was severely reduced, though it was later raised to the present limit of 21,000. When Rick Wright took over the club, he made further improvements by adding seats along the popular bank and in the enclosure. The Grandstand roof was also extended to give spectators greater protection in bad weather.

However, all these measures could not hide the outdated appearance of Ninian Park and it was clear that, to have a viable future, Cardiff City needed a new ground. Sam Hammam deserves the credit for setting the wheels in motion for a stadium and retail development across the road from Ninian Park. Unfortunately his plans proved to be too grandiose and, as the club's debts mounted, he was unable to persuade the Cardiff City Council to accept his business plan. When he resigned in 2006, the new Board of Directors at last succeeded in making the plans a reality, though on a reduced scale.

In years to come the new Cardiff City stadium will hopefully be the home of a Bluebirds team in the Premiership.

The stadium will now accommodate 27,000 spectators, though this figure could rise to 30,000 or more if Cardiff City can win promotion to the Premiership. It will be a home for the Cardiff Blues rugby team as well as the football club. People will be able to watch games in comfort with uninterrupted views wherever they are sitting.

As the Bluebirds prepare to move into a new stadium and a new phase in their history, City fans hope that it will herald a return to former glories. At the same time, as the curtain comes down on its final season, memories will live on of the stirring matches played at Ninian Park and the great players who have graced its turf. Soon nearly 100 years of history will come to an end and the ground will become another housing estate. It would be a fitting tribute to the stars of yesteryear if its streets proudly bear the names of those sporting heroes who gave us so much pleasure.

INDEX